Englisch

5./6. Klasse

First Steps

Ulrich Popko

First Steps

Hauptschwierigkeiten in den ersten beiden Lernjahren

INHALT

WAS MACHE ICH NUR FALSCH?

Hauptschwierigkeiten: Einführung

Hallo,

MacCool ist mein Name. Ich werde dich durch dieses Buch begleiten. Wie du eben bemerkt hast, habe ich angefangen, dich zu duzen. Dies ist unter Englischlernenden üblich, und so soll es auch zwischen uns sein, einverstanden?

Du hast vielleicht gerade mit dem Englischlernen begonnen oder bist schon im zweiten Lernjahr, und schon tauchen Schwierigkeiten auf. Kein Grund zur Panik, kann ich da nur sagen. Sprachen lernen heißt durch Fehler lernen. Was glaubst du wohl, wie viele Fehler ich machen würde, wenn ich eine Sprache lerne, die ich noch nicht fließend kann, z. B. Italienisch, Japanisch oder Arabisch? Wichtig ist nur, sich die Zeit zum regelmäßigen Üben zu nehmen. Dann werden die Fehler nach und nach seltener.

Nimm dir täglich 15–20 Minuten Zeit zum Üben.

Wenn du schon weißt, in welchen Bereichen der englischen Grammatik bei dir die meisten Fehler auftreten, umso besser. Dann suchst du dir das entsprechende Kapitel im Inhaltsverzeichnis und beginnst damit, machst dann mit dem nächsten „Fehler-Thema" weiter und so fort. Falls du aber nur eine ungefähre Ahnung von dem hast, was du falsch machst, beginne am besten mit dem Eingangstest auf Seite 10/11. Die Auswertung im Lösungsteil sagt dir dann, in welcher Reihenfolge du dieses Buch am günstigsten durcharbeitest.

Diagnosetest im dritten Kapitel

In den einzelnen Kapiteln wirst du dich leicht zurechtfinden. Auf der oberen Seitenhälfte findest du Regeln, Übersichten und Beispiele zu einzelnen Problemen. Es ist sehr wichtig, sie genau zu lesen, denn es gilt: Erst dann, wenn du verstanden hast, wo und warum Schwierigkeiten da sind, kannst du sie auch meistern. Übungen schließen sich an. Ich habe sie nicht zu lang gemacht, damit du nicht außer Atem gerätst und auch nicht dauernd auf die Uhr schauen musst. Ein Beispiel für eine Doppelseite aus dem Buch siehst du auf Seite 7.

Erledige die Übungen sorgfältig und vergleiche genau mit dem Lösungsteil. Falls dir unklar ist, warum du einen Fehler gemacht hast, lies nochmals den Regel- und Beispielteil durch. Wenn du grammatische Fachausdrücke nicht mehr genau kennst, schau einfach auf den Seiten 8 und 9 nach. Dort findest du eine Übersicht mit anschaulichen Erklärungen.

Du solltest dir ebenfalls ein Schreibheft anschaffen, in das du die Übungen einträgst, die mit dem Heftsymbol am Rand gekennzeichnet sind. Bei Übungen, die du im Buch erledigst, empfehle ich dir, Bleistifte und Buntstifte zu benutzen. Du kannst dann alles wegradieren und die Übungen später noch einmal machen.

Und nun viel Spaß und Erfolg bei der Arbeit!

Dein *MacCool*

Grammatische Fachausdrücke auf Seite 8/9

So sind die Doppelseiten dieser Lernhilfe aufgebaut:

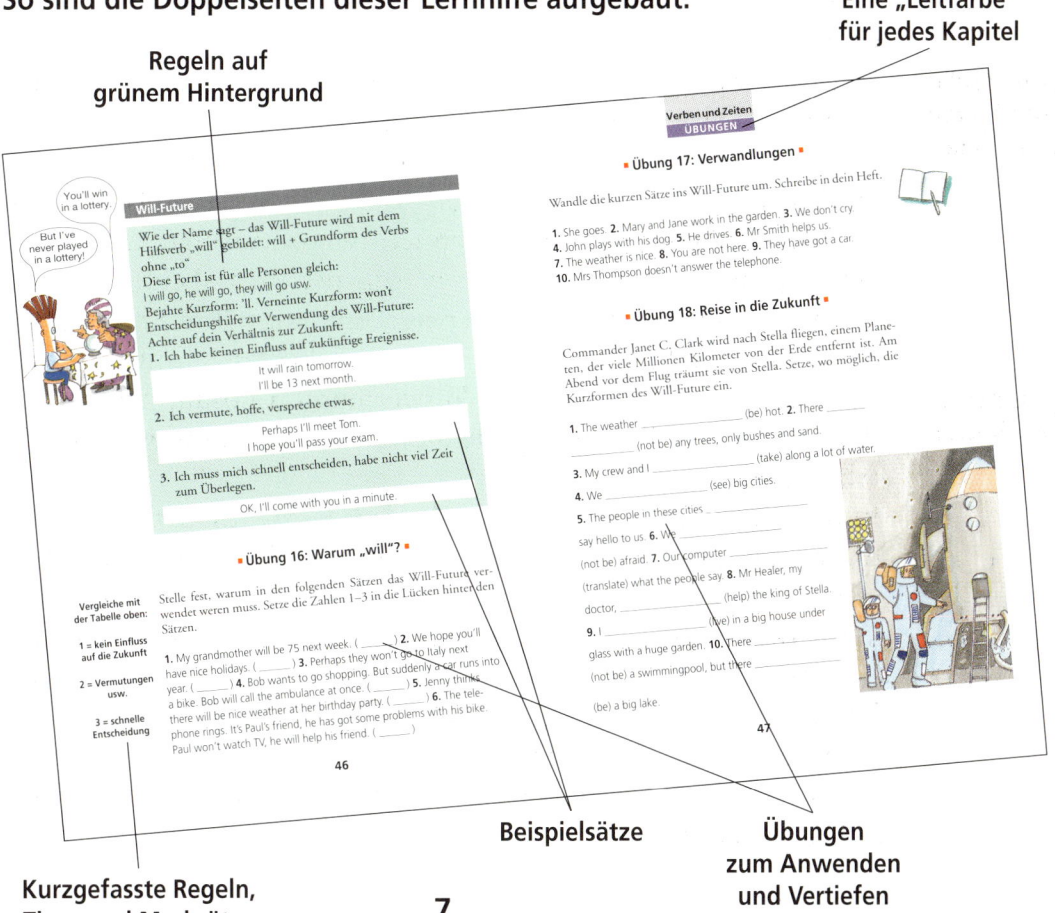

Regeln auf grünem Hintergrund

Eine „Leitfarbe" für jedes Kapitel

Kurzgefasste Regeln, Tipps und Merksätze

Beispielsätze

Übungen zum Anwenden und Vertiefen

WIE WAR DAS NOCH?

Wichtige grammatische Begriffe

Hier findest du wichtige grammatische Fachbegriffe, die in diesem Buch verwendet werden.

Adjektiv (adjective)

sagt aus, wie eine Person / Sache beschaffen ist; z. B. a **blue** pullover, a **big** tree; S. 60

Adverb der Art und Weise (adverb of manner)

sagt aus, wie eine Tätigkeit geschieht; z. B. Mr Miller is driving **carefully.** The boys and girls are singing **well.** S. 64

Ausführliche Erklärungen findest du auf den angegebenen Seiten.

Artikel, bestimmter (definite article)

begleitet ein Nomen; z. B. **the** car, **the** trees; S. 13

Artikel, unbestimmter (indefinite article)

geht ebenfalls einem Nomen voraus; z. B. **a** lake, **a** go-cart, **an** apple, **an** elephant; S. 13

Demonstrativpronomen (demonstrative pronoun)

weist auf etwas hin; z. B. **This** is my pen. S. 26

Die englischen Bezeichnungen sind eingeklammert.

Futur (will-future, going-to-future)

Zukunftsform des Verbs; z. B. I think it **will rain** tomorrow. We **are going to jog** a lot next week. S. 46, S. 48 / 49

Genitiv (genitive, possessive case)

Wesfall; sagt aus, wem etwas gehört: Janet**'s** new jeans, the Holdens**'** garden, the legs **of** the table; S. 16 / 17

Hilfsverb (auxiliary)

Verb, das zusätzlich zum Vollverb steht und z. B. hilft, die Verneinung oder eine Zeit zu bilden: He **does** not come. I **have** not seen her. S. 40

Komparativ (comparative)

Steigerungsform; zeigt z. B. an, ob etwas größer oder kleiner ist: Peggy is **taller** than Henry. S. 60

Kurzform (contracted form)
ist im Englischen bei Hilfsverben häufig; z. B. **doesn't, can't**; S. 40

Nomen, Substantiv (noun)
Hauptwort, Dingwort; z. B. ball, house; S. 12

Objekt (object)
Ergänzung zum Verb; z. B. They read **a book.** S. 58

Partizip Perfekt (past participle)
3. Verbform; z. B. to do, did, **done**; to play, played, **played**; S. 42

Perfekt (present perfect)
betont, dass eine Handlung irgendwann einmal stattgefunden hat;
z. B. She **has** already **done** her homework. S. 44

Personalpronomen (personal pronoun)
steht für eine Person oder Sache; z. B. I, he, it, we …; S. 22

Plural (plural)
Mehrzahl; z. B. books, boxes, hobbies; S. 14 / 15

Possessivpronomen (possessive pronoun)
zeigt den Besitz an; z. B. This is **her** bike. S. 24

Präsens (simple present, present simple)
Einfache Gegenwart; z. B. Norma **plays** tennis every Friday. S. 34

Präteritum, Vergangenheit (simple past, past simple)
weist auf eine abgeschlossene Handlung in der Vergangenheit hin;
z. B. They **made** a trip to New York last year. S. 38 / 39

Singular (singular)
Einzahl; z. B. book, box, hobby; S. 14 / 15

Subjekt (subject)
Wort / Worte des Satzes, nach dem / denen sich das Verb richtet;
z. B. **Helen** helps her parents. S. 58

Superlativ (superlative)
zeigt die höchste Steigerungsform an; z. B. Tom is the **greatest.** S. 60

Verlaufsform des Präsens (present continuous, present progressive)
zeigt an, dass gerade etwas passiert; z. B. She **is writing** a letter. S. 34

Vollverb
beschreibt eine Tätigkeit; z. B. drive, go, look, sing, think; S. 40

Präge dir die
Fachbegriffe
gut ein!

9

HÄTTEST DU'S GEWUSST?

Kleiner Eingangstest

Hier kannst du herausfinden, in welchen Bereichen der englischen Grammatik du Schwierigkeiten hast. Lies die Sätze genau durch, kreuze dann an, ob sie richtig oder falsch sind. Falls sie falsch sind, unterstreiche die fehlerhaften Worte. Vergleiche dann mit dem Lösungsteil und beachte die Lernhinweise.

Entscheide, was richtig oder falsch ist!

A
Nomen

B
Pronomen

R   F

1. This is a angry dog.

2. The childs are playing in the street.

3. Daniela has many hobbys.

4. Many peoples are in the street.

5. He wears a uniform.

6. Peters anorak is blue.

7. The Smiths' car is from France.

8. They go to the dentist's.

9. The children like english sweets.

10. The Kleins like American t-shirts.

11. Where are you from? – They are from Newcastle.

12. Where are the pupils' English books? –
They have left her books in the classroom.

13. This is Jerry's new cap. It's colour is blue.

14. This is his new friend.

15. Who is he? – My brother.

16. Who's book is that?

17. I can't see you. Where are you?

18. What sweat shirt do you like better,
the red or the yellow sweat shirt?

R   F

C

Adjektive

19. Robin was the goodest bowman.

20. This book is not so good as the book we read last time.

21. terrible – terribler – terriblest

22. funny – funnier – funniest

D

Verben und Zeiten

23. Who is comeing there?

24. He sayed hello when she came into the room.

25. We've seen a nice film last week.

26. She tooks a big bag with her.

27. Oh no! Jenny droped the new vase.

28. She did not go to London yet.

29. We can not help this poor man.

30. Pete has already helped him.

31. Kate is ill. She won't come to her friends' birthday party.

E

Fragen

32. Do you can help me?

33. May I open the window?

34. Who wear a blue cap?

35. Who do you live? In Swansea?

36. How many is that, please?

F

Wortstellung

37. At 8 o'clock went I home.

38. Do come you from France?

39. Our cat has every day milk.

40. You must report it to the police station.

G

Adverbien

41. They all are really happy.

42. The band played good.

43. The dog barked loudly.

44. She opened the door careful.

DEN DINGEN EINEN NAMEN GEBEN

Nomen / Nouns

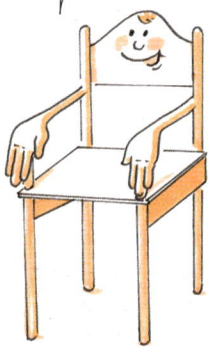

Hello, my name is chair.

Nomen

Das Wort **Nomen** kommt aus dem Lateinischen und bedeutet wörtlich „Namen". Nomen sind Namenwörter. Sie bezeichnen Dinge und Personen und antworten auf die Fragen:
- ▶ **Was** ist das? house, pen, ruler, biro, table, chair …
- ▶ **Wer** ist das? Mary, Dan, mother, father, sister, brother …

▪ Übung 1: Wo sind die Nomen? ▪

Male die Kästchen rot aus, in denen sich Nomen befinden. Schlage dann im Lösungsteil nach.

1.	Henry	plays	with	his	dog.
2.	We	are	at	school.	
3.	Mike	is	in	London.	
4.	My	sister	has got	a	hamster.
5.	My	parents	are watching	TV.	
6.	Where	is	Larry?		
7.	Linda	has got	a	new	bike.

▪ Übung 2: Welche Wörter sind Nomen? ▪

Unterstreiche in den folgenden Sätzen die Nomen und schreibe sie in dein Heft.

1. John says hello. **2.** The bird is on the table. **3.** Jack has got a red school-bag. **4.** Look, there is a taxi. **5.** The cat is under the sofa. **6.** The window is open. **7.** The water is in the glass. **8.** My father is in the house.

Nomen und Artikel

Nomen haben wichtige Begleiter, die Artikel!

	Bestimmter Artikel: the	Unbestimmter Artikel: a, an
Vor Konsonant (z. B. b, s, t)	Aussprache: / ð ə /	a / ə /
Vor Vokal (a, e, i, o, u)	Aussprache: / ð ɪ /	an / ən /

Nomen werden oft mit dem bestimmten oder unbestimmten Artikel verwendet:

/ ð ə / : the **t**eacher, the **r**oom, the **d**oor, the **t**axi

/ ə / : a **b**ike, a **d**esk, a **h**at, a **f**amily, a **d**og

/ ð ɪ / : the **o**range, the **e**vening, the **E**nglish teacher

/ ə n / : an **a**pple, an **o**ld man, an **e**xercise, an **e**mpty glass

Gefahr erkannt, Gefahr gebannt: Das „u" in uniform und unit wird behandelt wie ein Konsonant: a uniform, a unit.

▪ Übung 3: Welcher unbestimmte Artikel? ▪

Setze die richtigen unbestimmten Artikel ein.

1. This is _____ interesting book. **2.** Toby is _____ good dog. **3.** Look. I've got _____ very old hat. It's my grandfather's. **4.** Mr Bentley has got _____ old car. **5.** _____ blue box is on the table. **6.** There is _____ apple in the box.

▪ Übung 4: Leseübung ▪

Lies die folgenden Sätze. Kreuze die Sätze an, in denen „the" wie / ð ɪ / gelesen werden muss.

1. The pupils are happy, because school is over.
2. The old house looks nice.
3. Please open the window.
4. The old castle is on a hill.
5. The empty bucket is in a shed.

Nomen im Plural

Grundregel -s	nach Zischlaut -es	y nach Konsonant wird -ies
book → books	bus → buses	baby → babies
basket → baskets	box → boxes	diary → diaries
month → months	brush → brushes	family → families
table → tables	class → classes	hobby → hobbies
pen → pens	dress → dresses	*aber:*
car → cars		*toy - toys*
door → doors		

Wichtig: Bei Vokal + y bleibt „y" erhalten:
boy → boys
toy → toys

▪ Übung 5: Pluralformen ▪

Tipp:
Schau dir noch einmal genau die Tabelle oben an.

Schreibe die richtige Pluralform in dein Heft.

1. window, **2.** sister, **3.** country *(Land)*, **4.** boy, **5.** taxi, **6.** friend, **7.** girl, **8.** toy, **9.** bush, **10.** chip, **11.** diary *(Tagebuch)*, **12.** hamster, **13.** dress, **14.** kiss, **15.** hobby, **16.** shirt, **17.** river, **18.** teddy, **19.** bottle, **20.** circus

▪ Übung 6: Koffer packen ▪

In welchen Koffer gehören die Pluralformen? Ziehe Linien.
Beispiel: „Hotel" kommt in den Koffer mit „-s".

1. diary   **3.** book   **5.** brush   **8.** pencil   **10.** hammer
2. teddy   **4.** key   **6.** blouse   **7.** cowboy   **9.** pony

Übersicht: Unregelmäßige Pluralformen

Folgende Nomen bilden den Plural nicht durch einfaches Anhängen des „s" an die Singularformen:

Singular		Plural	Singular		Plural
man	→	men	sheep *(Schaf)*	→	sheep
woman	→	women	fish	→	fish
child	→	children	life	→	lives
foot	→	feet	potato *(Kartoffel)*	→	potatoes
mouse	→	mice	tomato	→	tomatoes
tooth *(Zahn)*	→	teeth	–		people

Hier noch etwas ganz Wichtiges: „Die Leute" heißt „people". Bitte kein „s" an people hängen! Es macht keinen Sinn.

Auch bei diesen Tieren Acht geben: **goose** *(Gans)* → **geese.**

▪ Übung 7: Abschlussübung zum Plural ▪

Schreibe die Pluralformen der Wörter in Klammern in die Lücken.

1. It's cold in this room, because all the _____ (window) are

open. **2.** Johnny is playing with his brother's _____ (toy).

3. The _____ (man)

and _____ (woman)

are talking about their _____

(child). **4.** The book has got

96 _____ (page).

5. Many _____ (family)

go on holiday in the summer.

6. There are six _____

(people) in the shop.

Der Genitiv drückt aus, wer der Besitzer einer Sache ist. Den S-Genitiv im Englischen erkennst du an der Schreibung **'s** (Apostroph und „s") oder nur **'** (Apostroph). Der S-Genitiv wird bei Personen (oder Tieren, zu denen ein gutes Verhältnis besteht) verwendet.

Der Genitiv gibt den Besitzer an.

> 1. **Jack's** bike is blue and yellow.
> 2. The **hamster's** new bed looks nice.
> 3. The **Holdens'** house is near a forest.
> 4. Go to the **dentist's** regularly.
> 5. "Bye, Mum, I'm at **Dan's**. We're playing basketball."

Im Singular wird **'s** angehängt (Sätze 1, 2, 4, 5), im Plural nur **'** (Satz 3). Der Apostroph + „s" an „dentist" (Satz 4) ist ein Überbleibsel aus früheren Zeiten, in denen gesagt wurde „dentist's house". „House" ist dann im Laufe der Zeit weggefallen. Dies ist auch in Satz 5 der Fall. „Dan's" bedeutet hier „bei Dan [zu Hause]".

▪ Übung 8: Wem gehört was? ▪

**Tipp:
Vergiss nicht den
Apostroph!**

Schreibe in dein Heft, wem die Dinge gehören.

1. Mr Smith – car. **2.** Mrs Jackson – sports car. **3.** Kate – exercise book. **4.** The hamster – food. **5.** Jenny – new trousers. **6.** The Ryans – caravan. **7.** The two budgies – cage. **8.** The grocer (Kaufmann) – children.

Der Of-Genitiv

Der Of-Genitiv wird bei Sachen verwendet. Er drückt aus, welche Sache wozu gehört.

> 1. The **door of the house** is green.
> 2. The **chairs of class 10** are new.
> 3. The **frame** *(Rahmen)* **of the go-cart** is strong.
> 4. The **pockets of the anorak** are warm.

Zur Luft gehört der Sauerstoff, zur Sache Genitiv mit 'of'.

In der deutschen Umgangssprache sagt man schon mal „Der Sohn von Herrn Schmidt". Versuche auf keinen Fall diesen Satz Wort für Wort aus dem Deutschen ins Englische zu übertragen. Im Englischen gilt: Den Of-Genitiv nur bei Sachen verwenden! Da Herr Schmidt eine Person ist, muss der Satz heißen: „Mr Schmidt's son".

■ Übung 9: Der störrische Computer ■

Der Übersetzungscomputer ist ins Stocken geraten. Hilf ihm beim Übertragen ins Englische. Schreibe die englischen Sätze in dein Heft.

Tipp: Überlege, ob die Dinge zu Personen oder Sachen gehören.

1. **Die Mutter von meinem Freund** is in the garden.
2. **Das Rad** *(wheel)* **des Gokarts** *(go-cart)* is too big.
3. **Der Comic meines Freundes** is good.
4. The classroom **von Paul** is nice.
5. I don't like **die Farbe** *(colour)* **seiner Socken** *(socks)*.

Groß- und Kleinschreibung

I love France!

Zum Glück braucht man sich im Englischen um weitaus weniger Regeln zu kümmern als im Deutschen. Grundsätzlich gilt: Fast alles wird kleingeschrieben.
Großgeschrieben werden:
► das erste Wort am Satzanfang
► Namen (Vor- und Zunamen, Namen von Städten, Flüssen, Bergen)
► das Personalpronomen „I"
► Länder und deren Bewohner und die dazugehörigen Adjektive, Sprachen; Schulfächer
► das „T" in T-Shirt; TV, CD, DJ
► Monatsnamen, Festtage.

1. **We** often play basketball. *(Satzanfang)*
2. My best friend is **Dan**. *(Vorname)*
3. He lives in **Liverpool**. *(Stadt)*
4. Sheila comes from **England**. *(Ländername)*
5. Hermann is John's **German** friend. *(Adjektiv zu Ländernamen)*
6. May **I** watch **TV** now? *(Personalpronomen „I" und „TV")*
7. Your **English** is good. *(Sprache)*
8. We like **Biology** *(Schulfach)*.
9. My **T-shirt** is white. *(„T" von T-Shirt)*
10. I haven't got enough money to buy that **CD**. *(„CD")*
11. Our summer holidays start in **July**. *(Monatsname)*
12. My grandma will be with us at **Christmas**. *(Festtag)*

▪ Übung 10: Großer oder kleiner Anfang? ▪

Setze die richtigen Wortanfänge der Nomen ein. Entscheide, ob groß- oder kleingeschrieben werden muss.

1. _____nglish; **2.** _____ugust; **3.** _____able; **4.** _____indow; **5.** _____hristmas;

6. _____-shirt; **7.** _____ook; **8.** _____iology

18

▪ Übung 11: Groß oder klein? ▪

Schreibe die Sätze in Groß- und Kleinschreibung in dein Heft.

1. MY NAME IS JENNY JENKINS. **2.** YOU KNOW, I COME FROM
SCOTLAND. **3.** MY MOTHER IS FROM GERMANY. **4.** WE ARE IN
TUTZINGEN NOW, A NICE LITTLE GERMAN TOWN. **5.** LOOK HERE!
THIS IS A T-SHIRT FROM TUTZINGEN. I LOVE IT.

▪ Übung 12: Das richtige Wort ▪

Finde das passende Nomen und entscheide, ob groß- oder kleingeschrieben werden muss.

Achtung:
Namen, Länder,
Länderadjektive,
Sprachen, T-shirt,
"I" dabei?

1. Everybody likes the new _____ (he plays CDs). **2.** It rains a lot in

_____ (11th month of the year). **3.** Joe hasn't got a _____

(something you write with). **4.** Children like _____ (25–12).

5. Where is the ruler? – It isn't in my _____

(you can put things into it and you can carry it)

6. Your _____ (a shirt which looks like a letter)

is really nice. **7.** I don't watch much _____

(a box which shows films) in summer.

8. Do you speak _____ (they speak it in Great Britain)?

▪ Übung 13: Abschrift ▪

Schreibe die Sätze ab und achte dabei auf Groß- und Kleinschreibung. Schreibe noch vier eigene Sätze dazu.

Tipp:
Deine eigenen
Sätze könnten
deine Eltern
korrigieren.

we are in france this year. it is august 15th. the weather is very sunny.
we swim a lot.

Nicht zählbare Nomen

Mengenangaben machen nicht zählbare Nomen zählbar.

Nicht zählbare Nomen im Englischen sind Nomen, vor die kein Zahlwort gesetzt werden kann. Im Deutschen gibt es auch solche Nomen, zum Beispiel „Milch". Du kannst nicht sagen: „Zwei Milche".

Nicht zählbare Nomen werden zählbar gemacht, indem anstelle der Zahlwörter Mengenangaben vor sie gesetzt werden. So kann man sagen:

two glasses of *(Mengenangabe)* milk

Übersicht: Nicht zählbare Nomen und Mengenangaben

Am besten, du lernst diese Ausdrücke sorgfältig.

Mengenangaben	nicht zählbare Nomen
a glass of, a bottle of	milk, lemonade, water
a cup of	tea, coffee
some, a lot of	sugar (Zucker)
some, a lot of	salt (Salz), pepper (Pfeffer)
a slice (Scheibe) of	bread, toast
a bar (Tafel) of, a square (Stück) of, a piece of	chocolate

▪ Übung 14: Wie viel? ▪

Was gehört zusammen? Ziehe Verbindungslinien!
Tipp: In einigen Fällen gibt es mehrere Möglichkeiten.

a bar of

three cups of

water

many

a bottle of

lemonade

five slices of

bread

some

tea

salt

two glasses of

a bucket of

milk

chocolate

children

21

DIE STELLVERTRETER

Pronomen / Pronouns

Pronomen und Personalpronomen

Pronomen sind Wörter, die **Nomen** im Satz vertreten.

Satz mit Nomen	Satz mit Pronomen
1. **Pam** is in the bus.	**She** is in the bus.
2. **The children** are playing football.	**They** are playing football.

3. **The boy** is swimming.	**He** is swimming.
4. **The house** has got eight windows.	**It** has got eight windows.

Du kannst nach den Nomen mit „wer" oder „was" fragen. Die Nomen sind Subjekte.

Die hervorgehobenen Nomen in der linken Tabellenspalte sind gleichzeitig Subjekte der Sätze. Pronomen, die Subjekte ersetzen, sind Personalpronomen.

Hier die Personalpronomen im Überblick:

„You" kann auch der Siezform im Deutschen entsprechen.

	Person	Pronomen	Übersetzung
Singular	1.	I	ich
	2.	you	du, Sie
	3.	he, she, it	er, sie, es
Plural	1.	we	wir
	2.	you	ihr
	3.	they	sie

▪ Übung 1: Ersetze die Nomen! ▪

Ersetze die unterstrichenen Satzteile durch die richtigen Personalpronomen. Schreibe die Sätze in dein Heft.

1. Look. <u>Miriam and Nina</u> are playing table-tennis.
2. There is Patrick. <u>Patrick</u> is playing with Hardy.
3. Cindy is here too. <u>Cindy</u> is Miriam's friend.
4. Where is the table-tennis ball?
    <u>The table-tennis ball</u> is under the table.
5. Where are Miriam and Nina now?
    <u>Miriam and Nina</u> are sitting at the table.
6. <u>Patrick</u> has got a glass of lemonade.
7. <u>The glass</u> is red and blue.
8. It is 5 o'clock now. <u>The children</u> are going home.

▪ Übung 2: Welche Personalpronomen? ▪

Setze die richtigen Personalpronomen in die Lücken ein.

1. Albert: Where is the red pencil? _____ isn't here.

2. The teacher: Are _____ Wendy, the new girl?

3. Wendy: Yes, _____ am Wendy from Hull.

4. Where are _____ from? – _____ are from Grimsby.

5. There are the Jacksons. _____ live in London.

6. Look at that car. _____ has got a tiger on the door.

7. There is Sharon. _____ is cleaning her bike.

8. Sharon's brother is here too. _____ is reading a comic.

9. There are children. _____ are playing in the street.

10. Where is Ben's mother? – _____ is in the garden.

23

This is **my** ice-cream!

Hilfsfragen:
Bin ich selbst
dabei? Spreche
ich andere an?
Spreche ich über
andere?

Possessivpronomen

	Singular	Plural	Meine Rolle
1.	my	our	ich bin dabei
2.	your	your	ich spreche an
3.	his, her, its	their	ich spreche über

Possessivpronomen zeigen an, wem etwas gehört. Lies die Beispiele aufmerksam durch!

1. This is not **your** book, it is **my** book.

2. I think it is **her** new pullover. **His** pullover is old.

3. Peter's go-cart. **Its** wheels are blue.

4. Are these **your** pencils? – No, here are **our** felt-pens.

5. Jack and Jane. **Their** bags are red and yellow.

▪ Übung 3: Welches Possessivpronomen? ▪

Tipp:
Sieh dir an, zu
welcher
Person/Sache
etwas gehört.

Setze die richtigen Possessivpronomen ein.

1. Where is _____ white T-Shirt, Mum? – It's on _____ bed.

2. Has John got a red school-bag? – No, _____ school-bag is blue.

3. Where are Jenny's sweets? – Bello, _____ dog has got them.

4. Where are _____ anoraks, Peter and Paul? – _____ anoraks?

Oh no! They are in _____ classroom. And now it's 6 o'clock!

5. James and Carol are at school. But _____ little brother is at home,

because he's ill. **6.** Look at the glass on Margret's table. _____ colours

are yellow, red and blue! **7.** I love the old house in Baker Street!

_____ garden is a hundred years old! **8.** There is Susan. _____

brother is a singer in a band. **9.** There is Robert. _____ sister is in

Germany now. **10.** Look at Sheila and John. _____ pullovers are dirty.

24

Some und any

I think I'm having some pizza today!

some	any
im bejahten Satz	im verneinten Satz
in Fragen (als Antwort wird „ja" erwartet)	in Fragen (Antwort „nein" oder unklar)

„Some" und „any" bezeichnen unbestimmte Mengen. Sie stehen vor zählbaren Wörtern im Plural (z. B. pupils, books) oder vor nicht zählbaren Wörtern (z. B. milk, bread). Sie werden aber auch mit „one / body", „thing" oder „where" zusammengesetzt: someone / somebody, anyone / anybody *(jemand)*; something, anything *(etwas)*; somewhere, anywhere *(irgendwo)*.

1. I think there is **some** *(etwas)* coke in the kitchen. *(bejahter Satz)*
2. There isn't **any** *(kein)* bread on the table. *(verneinter Satz)*
3. Is there **anybody** *(irgendjemand)* here? *(Frage, Antwort unklar)*
4. Is Darlington **somewhere** *(irgendwo)* in England?
   (Frage mit „ja" als Antwort)
5. **Some** *(einige)* children are playing in the street. *(bejahter Satz)*

▪ Übung 4: Some oder any? ▪

Entscheide, ob *some* oder *any* eingesetzt werden müssen.

1. There is _____ cake left from the birthday party. **2.** There aren't

_____ good tennis players in Jennifer's class. **3.** Can I have _____

fish and chips, please? **4.** We didn't see _____ ghosts at Belmore

castle. **5.** My Mum feels tired. She must have _____ tea, I think.

6. Where is my green pullover? It must be _____ where *(zusammen-*

geschrieben). **7.** It rained a lot yesterday. We couldn't see _____ body

(zusammengeschrieben) in the park. **8.** I'm afraid I haven't read

_____ thing *(zusammengeschrieben)* for my written test tomorrow.

25

Demonstrativpronomen

	nahe bei	weiter weg
Singular	this	that
Plural	these	those

Bedeutung:
diese(r)/jene(r);
dies hier/das dort

Demonstrativpronomen weisen auf Dinge hin, die nahe beim Sprecher oder weiter weg von ihm sind. Sie dienen auch dazu Dinge voneinander zu unterscheiden.

These mit langem
„i" bei vielen
Sachen/Leuten –
unter Garantie!

> **1. This** pullover is blue and **that** pullover is red.
> **2. This** book here is about dogs, **that** book there is about cats.
> **3. These** apples are red, **those** apples are green.

Bei Sätzen 1 und 2 stehen die Nomen im Singular (daher „this" / „that"), bei Satz 3 stehen die Nomen im Plural (daher „these" / „those").

▪ Übung 5: Auswahl ▪

Tipp:
Achte darauf,
wie weit die
Dinge vom
Sprecher entfernt
sind und ob
Dinge unter-
schieden werden.

Setze die richtigen Demonstrativpronomen ein.

1. _____ pullover here is too big for you, but _____ pullover is

OK. **2.** Oh look! Right here! Aren't _____ posters beautiful?

3. Just look over there! Can you see _____ beautiful flowers?

4. I like _____ green cap and _____ blue sneakers much better

than _____ black caps and _____ grey tennis shoes.

▪ Übung 6: Welches Demonstrativpronomen? ▪

Schreibe die richtigen Demonstrativpronomen vor die Nomen

Tipp:
Achte darauf, ob die Nomen im Singular oder Plural stehen.

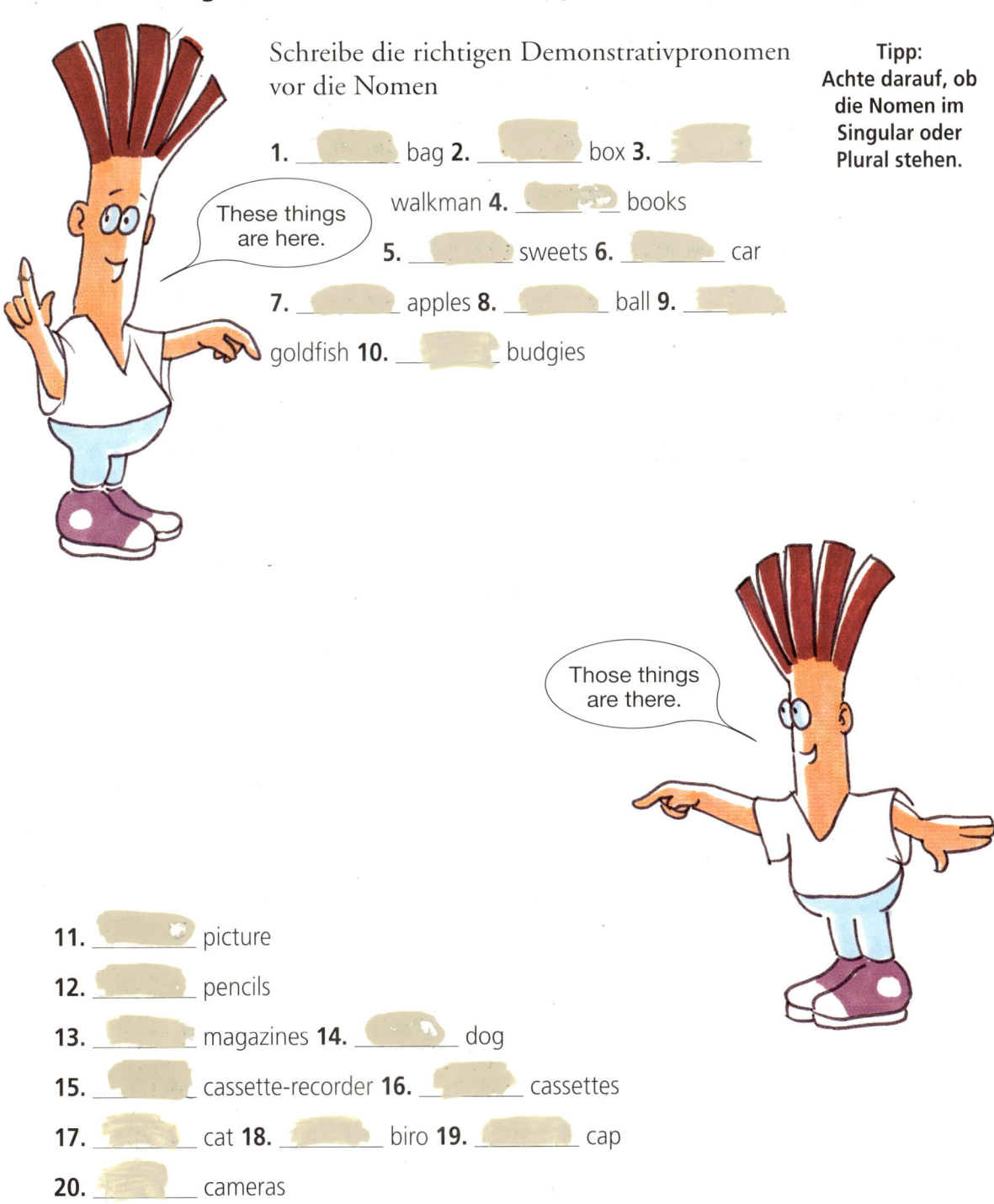

1. _____ bag 2. _____ box 3. _____ walkman 4. _____ books

These things are here.

5. _____ sweets 6. _____ car

7. _____ apples 8. _____ ball 9. _____ goldfish 10. _____ budgies

Those things are there.

11. _____ picture

12. _____ pencils

13. _____ magazines 14. _____ dog

15. _____ cassette-recorder 16. _____ cassettes

17. _____ cat 18. _____ biro 19. _____ cap

20. _____ cameras

Fragewörter

Fragewort	Frage nach:	Deutsche Bedeutung
who	Person	wer
what	Sache	was
whose	Besitz	wessen
how	Aussehen, Alter, Art und Weise	wie, auf welche Art und Weise
where	Ort	wo, wohin
when	Zeit	wann
why	Grund	warum

1. **Who** is that? – That's **Sandra.**
2. **What** have you got there? – **A new cassette** by the *Who.*
3. **Where** do you live? – I live **in Cambridge.**
4. **When** can you come back? – **On Tuesday.**
5. **Why** can't you come? – **Because** I'm ill.

▪ Übung 7: Welche Fragewörter? ▪

Setze die richtigen Fragewörter ein.

1. Your brother is not here. _____ is he? – No idea. **2.** _____'s your name? – My name is Joseph. **3.** _____ can you come? – I can come on Sunday. **4.** _____ dog is that? – It's Debby's dog. **5.** _____ old is Dan? – He's eleven. **6.** _____'s your telephone number? – It's 5-2-5-5. **7.** _____ often do you play tennis? – Every Monday. **8.** _____ can I do for you? – I need a blue pullover. **9.** _____ is John? – He's still at school. **10.** _____ is playing with us? – Mike, Sylvia and Eric. **11.** _____ long can we play? – For two hours. **12.** Sylvia, _____ bike is that? – It's my new bike.

What oder which?

what	which
wählt aus einer unbegrenzten Menge aus	wählt aus einer begrenzten Menge aus

Bedeutung: welche(r), welches

1. **What** can we do now? – Let's play table-tennis.
2. Mrs Mulligan has got two lollies. She asks Mary, „**Which** lollipop do you want to have?"

Satz 1 fragt nach irgendeiner Tätigkeit (Auswahl aus unbegrenzter Menge). Bei Satz 2 wird nach einer von zwei Möglichkeiten gefragt (Auswahl aus einer begrenzten Menge).

▪ Übung 8: What oder which? ▪

Setze das richtige der beiden Fragewörter ein. Achte genau auf die dargestellte Situation.

1. A reporter asks a film star, "_____ are you doing now? Are you making a new film?"

2. Joan shows two games to Annabel. She asks, "_____ game do you want to play?"

3. It is loud in Ben's room. Ben's mother asks, "_____ are you doing there, Ben?"

4. Dora and David are in a shop. The man in the shop asks, "_____ can I do for you?"

5. Susan shows two pictures to her brother. She asks, "_____ picture do you like better?"

6. In a bookshop. There are three books about horses. The shop assistant asks Mary, "_____ of them do you like?"

Hello, Mr MacCool.

Tipp: Zu Fragen gibt es noch ein Extrakapitel (Seite 50–53).

HALB SO SCHLIMM

Zwischentest I

▪ Aufgabe 1: Gleich mehrere ▪

Schreibe die Pluralformen der Tiere und Pflanzen unter die Bilder. Für jede richtige Lösung gibt es zwei Punkte.

Deine Punktzahl:

(1) ___

(2) ___

(3) ___

(4) ___

(5) ___

(6) ___

Summe: ___

1. _____   2. _____   3. _____

4. _____   5. _____   6. _____

▪ Aufgabe 2: Wem gehört was? ▪

Schreibe auf, wem was gehört. Verwende den richtigen Genitiv. Für jede richtige Antwort gibt es zwei Punkte.

Deine Punktzahl:

(1) ___

(2) ___

(3) ___

(4) ___

(5) ___

Summe: ___

1. Sharon – bike. _____

2. The Jacksons – car. _____

3. The windows – house. _____

4. Mr Miller – team. _____

5. The wheels – go-cart. _____

▪ Aufgabe 3: Ein Schlossgeist erzählt ▪

Setze die richtigen Wörter in die Lücken ein. Für jede richtige Lösung gibt es zwei Punkte.

Deine Punktzahl:

1. Hello, _____ name is Godfrey.

2. _____ 'm a ghost.

3. Look here! This is my castle. _____ 's 700 years old.

4. Many people are here in the summer. When I come into _____

   (ihre) rooms, I say hello to them.

5. Very often, _____ *(sie)* are afraid.

6. My sister is in Scotland. _____ *(ihr)* castle is small.

7. I always say to her, "_____ *(du)* don't work as much as I do."

This is my story.

(1) ___

(2) ___

(3) ___

(4) ___

(5) ___

(6) ___

(7) ___

Summe: ___

▪ Aufgabe 4: Bunte Mischung ▪

Setze die richtigen Wörter ein. Für jede richtige Lösung gibt es zwei Punkte.

Deine Punktzahl:

1. _____ is coming? – It's Fred.

2. _____ are Jane and Ken? – They're in the garden.

3. _____ is Mr Proper cleaning? – A window.

4. _____ ball has Timmy got, the red or the blue ball?

5. _____ are you watching TV? – Because the

   basketball match is interesting.

6. _____ do they get home? – At five o'clock.

Zur Auswertung schlage im Lösungsteil nach.

(1) ___

(2) ___

(3) ___

(4) ___

(5) ___

(6) ___

Summe: ___

WAS WANN TUN?

Verben und Zeiten / Verbs and Tenses

Bildung des Simple Present

Das Simple Present ist die **Grundform des Verbs ohne „to".**
In der dritten Person Singular (he, she, it) wird ein „s"
angehängt:

I come	we come
you come	you come
he, she, it com**es**	they come

Aufpassen musst du bei der Bildung der 3. Person Singular
auch wegen unregelmäßiger Formen:

**Achtung:
Ausnahmen bei
der 3. Person
Singular**

Nach Zischlauten → 'es' / ɪz /	wash → washes, miss → misses
Konsonant + 'y' → 'ies' / aɪz /	cry → cries, fly → flies
do, go, have	do → does /dʌz/ go → goes /gəʊz/ have → has

▪ Übung 1: Welche Endung? ▪

Füge die richtige Endung an.

**Tipp:
Manchmal ist
keine weitere
Endung
erforderlich.**

1. Sandra and Willy help_____ their father. **2.** Jack say_____ hello to
Jenny. **3.** She put_____ two glasses on the table. **4.** We sing_____ a
song. **5.** I understand_____ that. **6.** He go_____ home. **7.** The baby
cr_____. **8.** My uncle drive_____ a van. **9.** The children go_____ for
a walk with the dog. **10.** The dog run_____ after the cat.

Gebrauch des Simple Present

Das Simple Present ist eine Zeitform der Gegenwart. Es kennzeichnet Handlungen, die regelmäßig oder immer stattfinden. Oft weisen Signalwörter wie always, never, often, every auf solche Handlungen hin.

> **1.** They often go to the stadium to see their team.
> **2.** Dan never comes home late.
> **3.** Helen drinks a glass of milk every day.
> **4.** They always see their grandparents on Sunday afternoon.

Im Simple Present stehen ebenfalls Handlungen, die kurz aufeinander folgen.

> Dan puts on his shoes. He takes the football. He runs into the garden and shoots the ball. Petra shoots the ball back.

Folgende Verben werden *immer* im Simple Present gebraucht: love, like, want, understand.

> I play tennis every day.

▪ Übung 2: Tagein, tagaus ▪

Schreibe auf, was die Leute regelmäßig oder immer tun.

1. Jim / get up / at 6.30 / every day. **2.** The school bus / arrive at / 7.15.
3. School / start / at 8. **4.** He and his friends / have / lunch / at 11.30.
5. Becky / be / one of his best friends. **6.** After school / the two / play basketball in front of the house.

▪ Übung 3: Das 's' muss mit! ▪

Setze die richtigen Formen für die 3. Person Singular ein.

1. (go) _____ **2.** (fly) _____ **3.** (say) _____ **4.** (drive)

_____ **5.** (have) _____ **6.** (cry) _____ **7.** (be) _____

8. (do) _____ **9.** (have) _____ **10.** (watch) _____

Dies ist die Faustregel für die ing-Form. Ausnahmen auf der nächsten Seite.

Bildung des Present Progressive

Form von 'be' im Präsens + Grundform des Verbs + ing

I am reading	we are reading
you are reading	you are reading
he, she, it is reading	they are reading

Hilfsfrage: Was passiert gerade?

Gebrauch des Present Progressive

„Progressive" bedeutet so viel wie „andauernd, im Ablauf begriffen". Das Present Progressive ist eine Zeitform der Gegenwart. Es beschreibt Handlungen, die im Augenblick des Sprechens noch nicht zu Ende sind.

1. I can see Tim. He is washing his father's car.
2. There are Mary and John. They are helping their mother.
3. Where are you, Jack? – I'm in my room. I'm reading a book.

■ Übung 4: Was gehört zusammen? ■

Welche „progressive forms" passen in die Sätze? Ziehe Verbindungslinien, schreibe dann die Sätze in dein Heft.

1. Mrs Jackson – the newspaper. **2.** The children – TV. **3.** Jenny and Tom – table-tennis. **4.** I – my homework. **5.** Sandra – the door. **6.** The reporter – questions.

are playing

are watching

is reading

is opening

am doing

is asking

34

Übersicht: Abweichende Schreibung von ing-Formen

Stummes -e am Ende der Grundform	Konsonant nach kurzem, betontem Vokal
come → coming	stop → stopping
ride → riding	get → getting
cycle → cycling	sit → sitting
write → writing	run → running
live → living	win → winning
take → taking	begin → beginning
Das stumme -e fällt weg.	**Der Konsonant wird verdoppelt.**

Noch ein paar Ausnahmen:

tie → tying

die → dying

lie → lying

▪ Übung 5: Ausnahme oder nicht? ▪

Trage die richtige -ing-Form ein!

1. come _____

2. go _____

3. begin _____

4. take _____

5. sit _____

6. read _____

7. write _____

8. run _____

9. cry _____

10. shout _____

11. lie _____

12. cycle _____

▪ Übung 6: Welche Formen? ▪

Setze die richtigen Formen des Present Progressive der Verben in Klammern ein. Schreibe die Sätze in dein Heft.

1. Sandra – (write) – a letter to her friend. **2.** Three children – (play) – in the street. **3.** Sheila and Tim – (swim) – in the lake. **4.** Barbara – (kick) – the ball. **5.** The dog – (run) – after the cat. **6.** The boys and girls – (have) – a party. **7.** They – (dance). **8.** Jenny – (tie) – a string to her kite.

Zur Erinnerung:
Formen von 'be'
→ am, are, is

Present Progressive	Simple Present
Hilfsfrage: Was geschieht *gerade* und ist noch nicht zu Ende?	Hilfsfrage: Was geschieht *häufig, immer*? Was geschieht *kurz hintereinander*?
Signalwörter: just, now, at the moment, Look!	Signalwörter: always, often, never, every (day, week, month, year), sometimes, suddenly, then

▪ Übung 7: Bonny sorgt für Aufregung ▪

Sieh dir die Bilder und die darunter stehenden Stichworte genau an. Bilde dann jeweils Sätze zu jedem Bild und schreibe sie in dein Heft.

Tipp:
Stelle dir die Hilfsfragen der Tabelle oben. Achte auch auf das 's' in der 3. Person Singular.

1.

Look! Today – sun – shine.

Bonny – play – with the ball.

This – Bonny – Brenda's dog.

Bonny – like – the red ball.

3.

2.

Every day – Brenda and Bonny –

play – in the garden.

Brenda's mother – say –

„Please go to the supermarket

and buy some milk, OK?"

4.

Look! Brenda and Bonny –

walk – down the street.

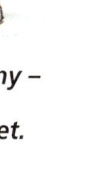

5.

Suddenly – Bonny – see – a cat.

Bonny – try – to catch it.

6.

The man on the bike – stop.

Now – apples and other things –

fall out of the basket.

The man – angry.

7.

A car – stop.

A woman – go over to Brenda.

The woman – angry, too.

8.

Bonny and the cat – come back.

The woman – happy.

She – say – to Brenda,

"This is Tilly, my cat.

I'm so happy."

Hinweis:
can, must, may
immer ohne 's',
niemals als
ing-Formen

9.

Brenda – say sorry – to the man.

The woman – laugh.

She – look – at her cat.

Grundform des Verbs ohne „to" + ed

> to clean → cleaned; to play → played, to open → opened;
> to shout → shouted

Bei Verben, die im Infinitiv auf -e enden, braucht nur ein -d angehängt zu werden:

> to cycle → cycled; to live → lived; to phone → phoned

▶ / d / nach Vokalen und stimmhaften Konsonanten (b, d, l, m, n, r) (cleaned, opened)
▶ / ɪd / nach / d / oder / t / (shouted)
▶ / t / nach gesprochenem stimmlosen Konsonanten (laughed, looked)

Besonderheiten gibt es in folgenden Fällen:

Puh!
Keine Regel ohne
„Besonderheiten"!

Endung Konsonant + y → -ied	Konsonantenverdoppelung nach betontem einfachen Vokal
to cry → cried	to stop → stopped
to carry → carried	to drop → dropped
to hurry → hurried	to nod → nodded

▪ Übung 8: Welche Endung? ▪

Bilde die Simple Past-Formen. Denke an die oben erklärten Besonderheiten.

1. to love _____ **6.** to drop _____

2. to empty _____ **7.** to cry _____

3. to stop _____ **8.** to collect _____

4. to count _____ **9.** to carry _____

5. to call _____ **10.** to cycle _____

Übersicht: Unregelmäßige Formen des Simple Past

to be, was/were	can, could	to catch, caught
to come, came	to do, did	to drive, drove
to fall, fell	to find, found	to get, got
to give, gave	to go, went	to have, had
to keep, kept	to leave, left	to pay, paid
to run, ran	to read, read	to say, said
to take, took	to think, thought	to write, wrote

Diese Tabelle ist nicht vollständig. Weitere Verben lernst du im Laufe der Zeit kennen. Übe sie!

Gebrauch des Simple Past

Das Simple Past ist eine Zeitform der Vergangenheit. Es berichtet über Ereignisse, die sich zu einer genau angegebenen Zeit in der Vergangenheit ereignet haben. Hilfsfrage: Was passierte wann genau?

Signalwörter: yesterday, last week/Sunday/month/year, in 1996, on 24th December, in the holidays

▪ Übung 9: Welche Zeit? ▪

Setze die richtige Zeit ein: Simple Present oder Simple Past.

Tipp:
Achte genau auf Signalwörter. Stelle dir Hilfsfragen.

1. Today, Rose _____ (be) at home. Yesterday, she _____ (be) in London. **2.** There she _____ (go) to Mme Tussaud's. **3.** She _____ (see) many famous pop stars. **4.** They _____ (look) like real people. **5.** In London last week, she _____ (have) her camera with her. **6.** She _____ (take) many photos. **7.** Now, at home, she often _____ (show) them to her friends. **8.** Rose _____ (visit) the Tower of London last Sunday. **9.** One day later, she _____ (do) some shopping. **10.** Now she often _____ (think) about London. London _____ (be) Rose's favourite city.

Bei der Verneinung ist die Unterscheidung zwischen Hilfs- und Vollverben wichtig. Folgende Hilfsverben kennst du schon: to be, to do, to have got, can, may.
Die anderen Verben wie to go, to write, to like sind Vollverben.

▶ **Verneinung von Hilfsverben:** Form des Hilfsverbs + not

Wichtig: 'cannot' ist *ein* Wort.

> I **am not (I'm not)** running.
> John **is not (isn't)** here.
> We **are not (aren't)** here today, we are in Bristol.
> They **cannot (can't)** come because they are ill.
> I **have got (I've got)** a new school-bag.
> She **has not got (hasn't got)** a glass of milk.

▶ **Verneinung von Vollverben:** Form des Hilfsverbs „do" + not + Grundform des Vollverbs ohne „to"

> They **do not (don't) write** letters, they write postcards.
> Janet **does not (doesn't)** like jazz, she likes pop music.

▪ Übung 10: Stimmt doch gar nicht! ▪

Behaupte das Gegenteil, indem du die folgenden Sätze verneinst. Nenne auch die Kurzformen.

Tipp:
Achte genau auf den Unterschied zwischen Hilfsverb und Vollverb.

1. Newcastle is in the USA. **2.** The Powells eat at a four-star restaurant every day.
3. Mary likes fish and chips. **4.** Pete has got a hamster. **5.** Pamela may go out until midnight. **6.** Tom collects stamps.
7. The Robertsons clean their car every day.
8. I eat a steak every day.
9. We have got five computers.

Verneinung des Simple Past

Hier gelten die gleichen Regeln wie bei der Verneinung im Simple Present. Einziger Unterschied: Anstelle der Präsensformen der Hilfsverben werden die Formen des Simple Past verwendet.

Formen des Hilfsverbs	Beispiele
am not, is not → was not (wasn't)	I **wasn't** in Newcastle.
are not → were not (weren't)	They **were not** at home.
have not/has not got → had not got (hadn't) got	We **had not got** the tickets. She **had not got** a pencil.
cannot → could not (couldn't)	They **could not** come.
do not, does not → did not (didn't)	I **did not write** to her. He **did not** arrive.

▪ Übung 11: Was ist richtig? ▪

MacCool hat alles falsch verstanden. Korrigiere ihn, indem du die Sätze verneinst. Schreibe in dein Heft. Nenne auch hier die Kurzformen.

1. Tom was at home yesterday.
2. Mary has got a new book.
3. The Watsons were in London last week.
4. Brenda watched TV yesterday.
5. Dan opened the door.
6. Jack bought a bag of sweets.
7. Pam is watching TV now.
8. Where was the key?
   They could open the door.
9. Janet can come with you.
   She must help me in the garden.
10. Mrs Pratt puts on the raincoat today, because the sun is shining.

Tipp:
Achte auf
Signalwörter und
den Sinn der
Sätze.

Präsensform von „have" + Past Participle (Partizip Perfekt)

Die Präsensformen von „have" + Past Participle	I/you have seen he/she/it has seen we/you/they have seen
Die Kurzformen von „have": 've und 's	I've closed the door. You've opened the window. He's washed the car.
Die verneinten Formen: have not (haven't) has not (hasn't)	They have not seen her. I haven't eaten the apple. She has not taken the bus. He hasn't cleaned the board.

Bei regelmäßigen Verben gibt es keinen Unterschied zwischen Partizip Perfekt-Formen und Formen des Simple Past (z. B. closed, cleaned, opened).
Bei unregelmäßigen Verben sind Partizip Perfekt-Formen und Simple Past-Formen meistens unterschiedlich (z. B. seen, come, taken).

Simple-Past-Formen siehe Seite 38/39.

▪ Übung 12: Setze die Kurzformen ein ▪

Tipp:
Die neuen Subjekte stehen in Klammern hinter dem Satz.

Wandle die Langformen in Kurzformen um. Schreibe die Sätze in dein Heft.

1. Pam and Helen have bought a bag of sweets. (They …) **2.** Helen has put them into her bag. (She …) **3.** They have gone to Tom and Dan. (They …) **4.** The girls and the boys have cycled 15 kilometres. (They …) **5.** But they have not been tired. (They …) **6.** They have stopped at a beautiful lake. (They …) **7.** Tom has not taken any photos. Too bad! (He …) **8.** He has not been happy about that. (He …) **9.** The children have had an excellent trip. (They …) **10.** They have not had any rain. (They …)

Übersicht: Unregelmäßige Formen des Past Participle

to be, was/were, been	can, could, *kein Past Participle*	to catch, caught, caught
to come, came, come	to do, did, done	to drive, drove, driven
to fall, fell, fallen	to find, found, found	to get, got, got
to give, gave, given	to go, went, gone	to have, had, had
to keep, kept, kept	to leave, left, left	to pay, paid, paid
to run, ran, run	to read, read, read	to say, said, said
to take, took, taken	to think, thought, thought	to write, wrote, written

Tipp:
Am besten, du lernst die Formen im „Dreier-Rhythmus" (Grundform, Simple Past, Past Participle), wie in der Tabelle angegeben.

▪ Übung 13: In die richtige Form bringen ▪

Wandle die Präsensformen in Present Perfect-Formen um. Verwende bei Flugzeug 1 Langformen, bei Flugzeug 2 Kurzformen. Schreibe die Formen in dein Heft.

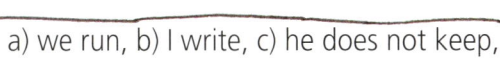
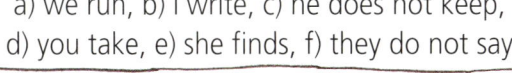

a) we run, b) I write, c) he does not keep,
d) you take, e) she finds, f) they do not say

a) I do, b) we think, c) he doesn't play,
d) she has, e) he doesn't fall, f) she gets

Das Present Perfect bezeichnet Handlungen, die zu einem nicht genau bezeichneten Zeitpunkt in der Vergangenheit stattgefunden haben und die für die Gegenwart wichtig sind. Folgende Signalwörter weisen auf das Present Perfect hin: already, just, lately *(neulich)*, not … yet *(noch … nicht)*.

> *Mother:* Where is your blue pullover?
> *Jack:* I don't know. I haven't found it yet.

Jack drückt mit seiner Antwort erstens aus, dass er irgendwann in der Vergangenheit (vor 10 Minuten, einer halben Stunde) nach seinem Pullover gesucht hat. Zweitens gibt er zu verstehen, dass der Pullover immer noch nicht da ist, er aber weitersucht.

Das Present Perfect weist auf zwei Dinge hin:
a) irgendwann in der Vergangenheit
b) Auswirkung auf die Gegenwart.

▪ Übung 14: Entscheidungen ▪

Tipp:
Achte auf Signalwörter.

Signalwörter zum Simple Past siehe Seite 39.

Kreuze an, ob die Handlungen zu einer bestimmten Zeit in der Vergangenheit ("PAST") stattfanden oder ob ein Bezug zur Gegenwart da ist ("NOW").

	Past	Now
1. Last Saturday, Daniela worked in the garden.	X	
2. "I've already done my homework. Can I play with Barbara now?"		X
3. Dot, Pam's dog, has brought back the little ball. Pam says, "Good, Dot."	X	
4. Bert is looking at photos from Brighton. He was there last summer.		X
5. When Fay broke her leg, she was in hospital for three weeks.	X	
6. "Oh no! What have you done with the milk? Look at your T-shirt!"		X

I haven't finished my homework yet.

44

▪ Übung 15: Was ist passiert? ▪

Schau dir die Bilder an. Schreibe auf, was die Personen gemacht haben. Benutze Langformen und schreibe die Sätze in dein Heft. Benutze die Verben in Klammern.

Tipp:
Achte auf den Unterschied have/has, beachte auch unregelmäßige Formen des Past Participle.

1. Look. There is Tom. He is putting his bike into the shed now. But what has Tom just done? (cycle)

_____

2. And here is Sheila. She is putting stamps on the letter now. But what has she just done? (write the letter)

_____

3. Margret and her friends are watching a basketball game on TV. But what have they done already? (play basketball)

_____

4. A taxi is waiting in front of Mrs Price's house. What has Mrs Price done? (call a taxi)

_____

5. Barky is tired. What has he done? (run after a cat)

_____

6. It is late. Janet is in bed now. What has she done before? (watch TV)

_____

45

You'll win in a lottery.

But I've never played in a lottery!

Will-Future

Wie der Name sagt – das Will-Future wird mit dem Hilfsverb „will" gebildet: will + Grundform des Verbs ohne „to"

Diese Form ist für alle Personen gleich:

I will go, he will go, they will go usw.

Bejahte Kurzform: 'll. Verneinte Kurzform: won't

Entscheidungshilfe zur Verwendung des Will-Future:

Achte auf dein Verhältnis zur Zukunft:

1. Ich habe keinen Einfluss auf zukünftige Ereignisse.

> It will rain tomorrow.
> I'll be 13 next month.

2. Ich vermute, hoffe, verspreche etwas.

> Perhaps I'll meet Tom.
> I hope you'll pass your exam.

3. Ich muss mich schnell entscheiden, habe nicht viel Zeit zum Überlegen.

> OK, I'll come with you in a minute.

▪ Übung 16: Warum „will"? ▪

Vergleiche mit der Tabelle oben:

1 = kein Einfluss auf die Zukunft

2 = Vermutungen usw.

3 = schnelle Entscheidung

Stelle fest, warum in den folgenden Sätzen das Will-Future verwendet werden muss. Setze die Zahlen 1–3 in die Lücken hinter den Sätzen.

1. My grandmother will be 75 next week. (_____) **2.** We hope you'll have nice holidays. (_____) **3.** Perhaps they won't go to Italy next year. (_____) **4.** Bob wants to go shopping. But suddenly a car runs into a bike. Bob will call the ambulance at once. (_____) **5.** Jenny thinks there will be nice weather at her birthday party. (_____) **6.** The telephone rings. It's Paul's friend, he has got some problems with his bike. Paul won't watch TV, he will help his friend. (_____)

▪ Übung 17: Verwandlungen ▪

Wandle die kurzen Sätze ins Will-Future um. Schreibe in dein Heft.

1. She goes. **2.** Mary and Jane work in the garden. **3.** We don't cry.
4. John plays with his dog. **5.** He drives. **6.** Mr Smith helps us.
7. The weather is nice. **8.** You are not here. **9.** They have got a car.
10. Mrs Thompson doesn't answer the telephone.

▪ Übung 18: Reise in die Zukunft ▪

Commander Janet C. Clark wird nach Stella fliegen, einem Plane-
ten, der viele Millionen Kilometer von der Erde entfernt ist. Am
Abend vor dem Flug träumt sie von Stella. Setze, wo möglich, die
Kurzformen des Will-Future ein.

1. The weather _____ (be) hot. **2.** There _____

_____ (not be) any trees, only bushes and sand.

3. My crew and I _____ (take) along a lot of water.

4. We _____ (see) big cities.

5. The people in these cities _____

say hello to us. **6.** We _____

(not be) afraid. **7.** Our computer _____

(translate) what the people say. **8.** Mr Healer, my

doctor, _____ (help) the king of Stella.

9. I _____ (live) in a big house under

glass with a huge garden. **10.** There _____

(not be) a swimmingpool, but there _____

(be) a big lake.

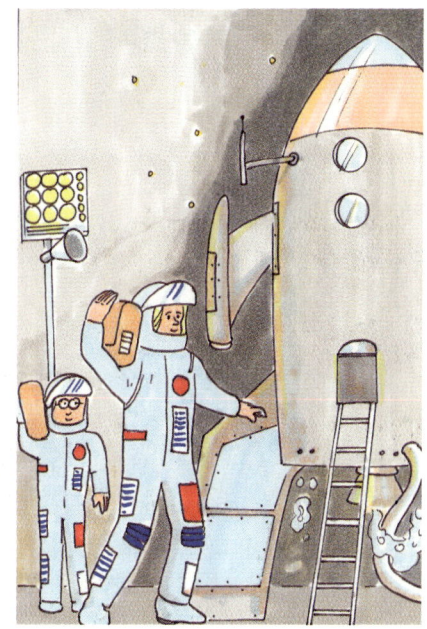

Going to-Future
bei:
– Absicht
– Vorhaben
– Plan

Das Going to-Future wird immer dann verwendet, wenn der Sprecher plant oder vorhat, etwas zu tun. Es beschreibt also beabsichtigte zukünftige Handlungen. Bildung:

Präsens von „be" + going to + Grundform des Verbs ohne „to"

I am going to eat	we are going to eat
you are going to eat	you are going to eat
he, she, it is going to eat	they are going to eat

It is John's plan to go to New York in April.
→ John is going to go to New York in April.

■ Übung 19: Zu erledigen ■

Hier siehst du Debbies Notizzettel. Darauf steht in knapper Form, was sie für den Nachmittag plant. Setze das Going to-Future ein und schreibe die Sätze in dein Heft.

7 o'clock: TV → At seven o'clock Debbie is going to watch TV.

1. This afternoon: buy a birthday present for Caren.
2. At five o'clock: tidy up my room.
3. Tomorrow: repair Ben's bike.
4. At the weekend: be at my grandparents'.
5. Next Monday: play football.
6. Today at six o'clock: help my mother in the kitchen.

Will-Future	Going to-Future
kein Einfluss auf Ereignisse	Absicht
Hoffnung, Vermutung	Vorhaben
schnelle Entscheidung	Plan

Noch einmal wichtige Unterschiede in Kurzform. Genaueres auf Seite 46 und 48.

▪ Übung 20: Welches Futur? ▪

Entscheide, ob das Will-Future oder das Going to-Future eingesetzt werden muss. Gebrauche, wenn möglich, Kurzformen und setze die Langformen in Klammern dahinter.

Tipp: Achte genau auf die vorgegebene Situation.

1. Mrs Palmer says to her son, "Please don't forget your raincoat.

It _____ rain tomorrow." **2.** Jenny says to

her friend, "Sorry, I can't come tomorrow, because I _____

_____ go to my uncle's. He invited me last week."

3. The "Sheffield Stars" lost their basketball match last weekend.

One week later, after the training, their coach says, "I hope you

_____ win the next match."

4. Mrs Putnam says to her neighbour, "When we went to France last

year, the weather wasn't good. We hope this summer the weather

_____ be much better." **5.** What are Paul's

plans for tomorrow? He _____ play tennis.

6. Sally looks at her notebook. She and her brother _____

_____ see the Tree-House Boys in concert.

7. Howard says, "My German homework is really difficult. Sorry, but I

_____ come to your party a little bit later."

Merken!
Bei Vollverb in der Frage do/does verwenden.

NOCH FRAGEN?

Fragen und Antworten / Questions and Answers

Fragen mit do

Im Deutschen stellst du Fragen, indem du das Verb vor das Subjekt setzt:

> **1. Spielst** *(Verb)* **du** *(Subjekt)* Fußball?
> **2.** Wann **kommt** *(Verb)* **er** *(Subjekt)* nach Hause?

Im Englischen musst du eine Form von „do" verwenden:

Diese Frageform funktioniert nur mit Vollverben (Spalte 3).

Form von „do"	Subjekt	Grundform des Verbs ohne „to"	Rest des Satzes
1. Do	you	**play**	football?
2. When **does**	he	**come**	home?
3. Does	she	**like**	milk?

Die Form von „do" richtet sich nach dem Subjekt (Spalte 2). Das Vollverb (Spalte 3) steht in der Grundform ohne „to". Sind die **Hilfsverben** „be", „have got", „can" im Fragesatz, so verwende keine Form von „do".

Keine Form von ‘do’ bei den Hilfsverben ‘be’, ‘have got’, ‘can’

> **1. Is** Janet at home?
> **2. Have** you **got** a pen for me?
> **3. Can** Mara **play** the guitar?

▪ Übung 1: Bilde Fragen ▪

Bilde aus den Aussagesätzen Fragen.

Tipp:
Beachte, ob ein Hilfsverb im Satz steht.

1. Robert plays football. **2.** The girls go to Glasgow. **3.** The children read many books. **4.** Robert can play the piano. **5.** Mildred is here. **6.** Betty likes cats.

Fragen mit what und who

Verwendest du die Fragewörter „who" (wer) oder „what" (was), so gilt:

▶ Sind who/what **Subjekt** des Fragesatzes, dann verwende **keine Form von „do"**.

> **1. Who** *(Subjekt)* **helps** *(Verb)* Mrs Norton every Monday?
> **2. What** *(Subjekt)* **flies** *(Verb)* through the air?

▶ Sind jedoch andere Wörter als „who" oder „what" Subjekt im Fragesatz, dann läuft alles ganz normal. Verwende eine Form von „do" bei Verben außer „be", „have got" und „can":

> **1.** Who do **you** *(Subjekt)* help every Monday?
> **2.** What does **Sheila** *(Subjekt)* read?
> **3.** What can **you** *(Subjekt)* see there?
> **4.** Who does **she** *(Subjekt)* visit on Sundays?

Heißt das Subjekt 'what' oder 'who', dann verwende niemals 'do'.

▪ Übung 2: Ein Reporter fragt ▪

Fred, Reporter für den „Daily Star", fragt bei einer Pressekonferenz genau nach. Schau dir Freds Notizen an und stelle Fragen.

1. The President: play the guitar.
2. His wife: work in the garden every day.
3. His children: get up every morning at 6 o'clock.
4. The President's parents: live in Memphis.
5. President: fly to Paris every year (why).
6. The President's friends: eat at a party (what).
7. The President's daughter: ride a horse.
8. The President and his wife: like Country & Western music.
9. The President: can speak German and French.
10. The President: eat when there is a meeting (what)

Kurzantworten

Falls du einige Begriffe nicht mehr kennst, dann schlage nach auf Seite 8/9.

Im Englischen gilt es als unhöflich, auf eine Frage nur mit einem knappen Ja oder Nein zu antworten. Vom Befragten wird erwartet, noch kurz auf die Frage Bezug zu nehmen:

> **1.** Is *(Hilfsverb)* Joan at home? – Yes, she is.
> **2.** Can *(Hilfsverb)* Robin and Clare speak Spanish? – No, they can't.
> **3.** Do *(Form von 'do')* the children play cricket? – No, they don't.
> **4.** Does *(Form von 'do')* he watch TV every day? – Yes, he does.

In der Kurzantwort greifst du also das Subjekt wieder auf und hängst außerdem das Hilfsverb oder eine Form von to do an.

Personal-pronomen – kein Problem!

I they
you you
he
we it
she

Verb im Fragesatz	Verb in der Kurzantwort
Fragesatz enthält Hilfsverb	Yes / No + Personalpronomen + Form des Hilfsverbs
Fragesatz enthält Form von 'do'	Yes / No + Personalpronomen + Form von 'do'

▪ Übung 3: Kurz und bündig ▪

Tipp: Achte genau auf Verben und Personen im Fragesatz.

Gib Kurzantworten.

1. Is Jimmy at home? No, _____

2. Can Peggy and her friends go to the cinema? Yes, _____

3. Is Hans from Germany? Yes, _____

4. Does Jenny feed her hamster? No, _____

5. Are the children in their room? Yes, _____

6. Do Pat and Pete like fish and chips? No, _____

7. Can Toby have some ice-cream? Yes, _____

Pronomen in Kurzantworten

In den Fragen auf der vorigen Seite wird über Personen gesprochen. Die Wahl des Pronomens in der Kurzantwort ist daher einfach: Du ersetzt das Subjekt in den Fragen durch das Pronomen.

> Does Jack see his friends? – Yes, he does.

Es gibt jedoch auch Fragen, in denen jemand direkt angesprochen wird. Dann musst du in der Kurzantwort entweder „I", „we" oder „you" wählen.

> **1.** Are you at home, Christine? – Yes, I am.
> **2.** Have you got pets, Bob and Helen? – Yes, we have.
> **3.** Can we go now, Mrs Morgan? – Yes, you can.

Can I give you a lift?

Yes, you can.

▪ Übung 4: Mehr Kurzantworten ▪

Welche Antwort gehört wohin? Ordne sie den Sätzen unten zu.

we do   we are   they do

       she does   we aren't

   he doesn't

          I'm not   they are

1. Does Anne understand German? – Yes, _____

2. Tim and Sheila, are you afraid of ghosts? – No, _____

3. Are the children watching tennis on TV? – Yes, _____

4. Thomas, are you from Essen in Germany? – No, _____

5. Do the boys like milk? – Yes, _____

6. Are you waiting for the bus, Melanie and Toby? – Yes, _____

7. Does Mike wear a hat? – No, _____

8. Do we put on our old jeans? – Yes, _____

MAL SEHEN

Zwischentest II

▪ Aufgabe 1: Was passiert gerade? ▪

Deine Punktzahl:

(1) ___

(2) ___

(3) ___

(4) ___

(5) ___

(6) ___

Summe: ___

Schreibe auf, was gerade geschieht. Verwende das Present Progressive und schreibe die Sätze in dein Heft.
Für die richtige Form von 'be' und für die ing-Form gibt es je einen Punkt.

1. Kate – ride a horse. **2.** The train – stop at the station. **3.** You – write a letter? **4.** Tommy says, "It's ten o'clock in the evening. I – get tired."
5. Jenny asks, "What – lie there?" **6.** The children are happy, because they – have a party.

▪ Aufgabe 2: Welche Endung? ▪

Deine Punktzahl:

(1) ___

(2) ___

(3) ___

(4) ___

(5) ___

(6) ___

(7) ___

(8) ___

(9) ___

(10) ___

Summe: ___

Setze die richtigen Verb-Endungen des Präsens ein. Tipp: Manchmal wird das Simple Present verwendet, manchmal das Present Progressive. Pro Lücke gibt es einen Punkt.

1. The telephone is ring_____. **2.** Cindy answer_____ the telephone. **3.** She says, "Hello, can_____ I help you?" **4.** Her friend Diana is talk_____ to her. **5.** She want_____ to invite Cindy to a party next Saturday. **6.** Cindy like_____ the idea. **7.** Then she ask_____, "Who is com_____?" **8.** Diana answer_____, "My friends from school want_____ to come." **9.** When Cindy hear_____ this, she say_____, "O.K., I'm coming." **10.** It is Saturday afternoon. Cindy is danc_____. She like_____ the party.

Aufgabe 3: Ein Picknick ■

rogressive oder das Simple Present ein. Pro Lücke
t.

_____ (shine). **2.** The Hansons _____ (have)

a picnic. **3.** Eric and Tara, their children, _____ (ask) them,

"May we play frisbee?" **4.** "Sure, no problem," _____ (say)

Mr Hanson. **5.** The children _____ (take) their frisbees and

_____ (go) away, but not too far – just 100 metres.

6. Tara _____ (throw) the frisbee first. **7.** She and her brother

sometimes _____ (throw) the frisbee high into the air.

8. Look! They _____ (have) a lot of fun. **9.** Now Eric's frisbee

_____ (fly) like a bird. **10.** Oh no! It _____ (swoosh)

over a fence and then _____ (land) on the back of a bull.

11. The bull _____ (get) very angry. **12.** It _____ (run)

to the fence. **13.** The children

_____ (run) away.

14. But then they

_____ (can) hear

a voice from behind,

"Don't run away, children."

15. Tara and Eric _____

(look) around. **16.** A farmer _____ (have) got their frisbee.

17. He _____ (say) to them, "I'm afraid you can't _____ (play)

frisbee with Bully." **18.** Then he _____ (give) them the frisbee.

▪ Aufgabe 4: Die richtige Zeit ▪

Setze Simple Present, Present Progressive, Present Perfect oder Simple Past ein. Verwende Langformen. Pro richtige Verbform gibt es einen Punkt.

1. Today, it _____ (be) Janet's birthday. **2.** She _____ (be) twelve years old. **3.** She _____ already _____ (invite) her best friends: Jack, Joan, Clare and Tom. **4.** She _____ (send) them a nice card. **5.** She _____ (make) it on her father's computer two weeks ago. **6.** Now it _____ (be) three o'clock in the afternoon. **7.** Her friends _____ (wait) at the front door. **8.** Now they _____ (say) hello to Janet. **9.** They _____ (give) her a book about horses and a cassette by the Main Street Boys, Janet's favourite pop group. **10.** Janet really _____ (like) them. **11.** Last week, her friends _____ (ask) themselves, "What is the right present for Janet?" **12.** Now they _____ (know) that they _____ (buy) the right present for her.

▪ Aufgabe 5: Zukunftspläne ▪

Bilde Sätze und schreibe sie in dein Heft. Entscheide, ob du das Going to-Future oder das Will-Future einsetzen musst. Pro Satz gibt es einen Punkt.

Steve has finished his school education. He has made some plans for the future:
1. He – visit – his uncle in Germany. **2.** There he – work – at his computer firm. **3.** Steve – learn – how computers work.

Steve also wonders about a lot of things:
4. I – be – very happy? **5.** I – meet – a nice girl? **6.** I – win – in the lottery?

56

▪ Aufgabe 6: Richtig fragen – kurz antworten ▪

Setze die richtigen Fragewörter ein. Gib richtige Kurzantworten. Benutze, wann immer es geht, Kurzformen. Pro Satz gibt es einen Punkt.

Mrs Johnson and her family were in Spain last summer. A reporter is asking Mrs Johnson some questions.

Deine Punktzahl:

1. "_____ did you go last summer?" – "We went to Spain."

(1) ___

2. "Was the weather O.K.?" – "Yes, _____." **3.** "_____ did you

(2) ___

do there?" – "We went swimming, we visited Barcelona, we also went

(3) ___

dancing." **4.** "Did you also go sailing?" – "No, _____. – You know,

(4) ___

we always get seasick." **5.** "Did you like it in Spain?" – "Oh yes,

_____. You know, the people there were very kind." **6.** "Don't

(5) ___

you feel sad now – no sun, too much rain?" – "No, _____."

(6) ___

7. "_____ are you happy now?" – "Because we can meet all our

friends." **8.** The reporter and Mrs Johnson can hear a loud noise. Mrs

(7) ___

Johnson asks, "_____ dog is that? He's running after our cat. Sorry,

(8) ___

but I have to go now."

Summe: ___

Die Plaza de Cataluna in Barcelona

VORSICHT, BAUSTELLE!

Satzbau / Sentence Structure

Ein englischer Satz mit Niveau hat immer S-P-O.

Wortstellung im Satz

Sicher hast du schon einmal von englischen Muttersprachlern Sätze wie diesen gehört: „Gestern ich spielte Tennis." Wir verstehen zwar, was gemeint ist, sind aber sicherlich nicht einverstanden mit der Aufeinanderfolge der Worte im Satz. Aber: Diese Wortstellung ist im englischen Satz richtig. Es gilt die S-P-O-Regel, also Subjekt-Prädikat (Verb)-Objekt:

Subjekt	Prädikat / Verb	Objekt
I	play	tennis.
He	watches	TV.
Mrs Sears	has got	a white cat.

Andere Satzteile werden hinter das Objekt oder vor das Subjekt gesetzt, also

I play tennis on Monday. On Monday, I play tennis.
He watches TV on Saturday.

▪ Übung 1: Bilde richtige Sätze ▪

Die folgenden Satzteile sind durcheinander angeordnet. Schreibe sie in der richtigen Reihenfolge in dein Heft.

1. a nice new blouse – has got – Jennifer **2.** to them – they talk
3. John – with – is playing – his dog **4.** reading – a book – is – Anne
5. a party – are – the children – having **6.** on – has got – her new cap – Jenny **7.** schoolchildren – British – many – school uniforms – wear
8. does – like – not – dog biscuits – Snuffy

Satzteile

Ein vollständiger Satz muss mindestens ein Subjekt und ein Verb haben. Ein Objekt ist nicht immer erforderlich. Viele Sätze haben auch noch Orts- oder Zeitbestimmungen. Sie antworten auf die Fragen: Wo? Wohin? Wann?

> **1.** Tony laughs. *(Nur Subjekt und Verb, kein Objekt)*
> **2.** Marita goes to Sheffield. *(Subjekt, Verb und Ortsbestimmung)*
> **3.** Tom gets up at 7.30. *(Subjekt, Verb und Zeitbestimmung)*
> **4.** Paula and her team play football in the stadium on Friday.
> *(Subjekt, Verb, Objekt, Ortsbestimmung, Zeitbestimmung)*

Wenn in einem Satz Orts- und Zeitbestimmung vorkommen, so gilt: **Ortsbestimmung vor Zeitbestimmung.**

Nicht vergessen: Verb und Objekt gehören zusammen, kein Wort dazwischenschieben!

Bei Orts- und Zeitbestimmungen richte dich nach dem Alphabet: O vor Z.

▪ Übung 2: Sätze, Sätze ▪

Bilde mit den untenstehenden Stichworten Aussagesätze (keine Fragesätze). Beachte die Satzbauregeln. Schreibe die Sätze in dein Heft.

Tipp: Übertrage die Tabelle in dein Heft, schreibe die Satzteile in die richtigen Tabellenspalten.

Subjekt	Verb	Objekt	O	Z

1. play basketball – in the evening – MacCool
2. Mr Paulsen – in the hotel – watched TV – in the evening **3.** in the afternoon – Pat – in the kitchen – helps her father **4.** every evening – eat – the Wilsons – an apple **5.** cycles – Christine – along the river – in the afternoon **6.** Mrs Paulsen – a letter – wrote – in the evening – in the living-room **7.** Mr Jennings – at the pictures – looked – on the table – after lunch **8.** Sarah and Toby – put – on the table – a bottle of milk – after shopping **9.** to the park – Mrs Potter – went – with her dog – in the afternoon **10.** at 10 o'clock – sang a song – the children in 6c

SO SIEHT'S AUS

Adjektive / Adjectives

Steigerung der Adjektive

Steigerung mit -er / -est	Beispiele
Einsilbige Adjektive	loud, louder, loudest great, greater, greatest
Einsilbige Adjektive mit betontem einfachen Vokal: Verdoppelung des Endkonsonanten	fat, fatter, fattest wet, wetter, wettest flat, flatter, flattest
Zweisilbige Adjektive mit y-Endung: „y" wird zu „ie"	funny, funnier, funniest silly, sillier, silliest

Steigerung mit more, most	Beispiele
Zweisilbige Adjektive ohne y-Endung	careful, more careful, most careful
Adjektive mit mehr als zwei Silben	fantastic, more fantastic, most fantastic

▪ Übung 1: Welche Steigerungsform? ▪

Finde die richtigen Steigerungsformen zu den Adjektiven.

1. big _____

2. tall _____

3. modern _____

4. hungry _____

5. thin _____

6. famous _____

*Bild rechts:
William
Shakespeare –
the most famous
British poet*

Vergleich

▶ **Gleiche Dinge werden verglichen:**
as + Grundform des Adjektivs + **as**

gleiche Dinge:
as ... as

> **1.** Harry is **as** tall **as** Jack.
> **2.** Joan's bag is **as** heavy **as** Petra's bag.
> **3.** The music in Miriam's room is **as** loud **as** the music
> in her brother's room.

▶ **Ungleiche Dinge werden miteinander verglichen:**
Komparativ + **than**

ungleiche Dinge:
... than

> **1.** Christine is tall**er than** Sam.
> **2.** Helen's story is **more** interesting **than** Jenny's story.
> **3.** William's box is bigg**er than** Oscar's box.

▪ Übung 2: Vergleiche ▪

Vergleiche, was du auf den Bildern sehen kannst. Schreibe die Sätze in dein Heft.

1. Spot's house – big – Fang's house

2. Suzy – not wet – Flag

3. The water – hot – the lemonade

4. A lion – dangerous – a cat

5. London – big – Berlin

Tipp:
Im Zweifelsfall
auf Seite 60
nachschlagen.

Achtung –
manche Adjektive
werden unregel-
mäßig gesteigert!

Übersicht: Unregelmäßige Steigerung der Adjektive

Grundform	Komparativ	Superlativ
good	better	best
bad	worse	worst
much, many	more	most
little, small	smaller	smallest

1. Mary is a good swimmer, John is better than Mary, and Joan is the best swimmer.

2. Jim has got a small piece of chocolate. Greg's piece is smaller, Sylvia has got the smallest piece.

▪ Übung 3: Viele Formen ▪

Trage die fehlenden Formen in die Tabelle ein.

Grundform	Komparativ	Superlativ
short		
	younger	
		best
small		
funny		
hot		
		worst
	more dangerous	
terrible		
		luckiest
wet		
famous		

▪ Übung 4: Zwei Städte im Vergleich ▪

Emlyn und Flora, zwei junge Marsbewohner, sehen sich zwei irdische Städte an. Dabei stellen sie einige Unterschiede fest. Sie machen sich Notizen, benutzen dabei folgende Abkürzungen: (o) Grundform; (+) Komparativ, (NY) New York, (V) village, (→) Hinweis, (/) Vergleich zu.
Forme die Marsnotizen zu Sätzen um und schreibe die Sätze in dein Heft.

Beispiel: V: shops → small (+) / NY
In the village, shops are smaller than in New York.

Links:
New York,
Times Square

Rechts:
Die Kleinstadt
Arundel in
Sussex

1. NY: houses → high (+). **2.** NY: cars → many (+). **3.** NY: streets → noisy (+), dirty (+). **4.** V: people → poor (+). **5.** NY: shops → big (+) / V. **6.** V: streets → quiet (+). **7.** NY: not exciting (o) / village. **8.** V: trees → many (+) / NY. **9.** V: streets → not wide (o) / NY. **10.** V: people → friendly (+) / NY.

Tipp:
Manchmal musst du auch there is / there are verwenden.

WIE'S GETAN WIRD

Adverbien der Art und Weise / Adverbs of Manner

Adverbien der Art und Weise

Hilfsfrage:
Wie (auf welche Art und Weise) handeln die Personen, geschieht etwas?

Adverb bedeutet wörtlich „beim Wort". Adverbien der Art und Weise stehen bei der Wortart Verben. Sie geben an, **wie** etwas geschieht. Im Englischen haben Adverbien in der Regel die Endung -ly.

> **1.** Why hasn't the train arrived yet?
> Mrs Wilson looks **nervously** at her watch.
> **2.** "We love ice-cream!" the children shout **excitedly.**
> **3.** Paul has a pain in his left leg. He walks **slowly** down the street.

Keine Regel ohne Ausnahme!

Bildung von Adverbien

Wie du an den Beispielen sehen kannst, nimmt man zur Bildung der Adverbien das **Adjektiv** und hängt die **Endung -ly** an. Es gibt jedoch Ausnahmen:

l → lly	le → ly	y → ily
awful → awfully	terrible → terribly	happy → happily
careful → carefully	possible → possibly	angry → angrily

Das Adverb zu „good" heißt „well".

▪ Übung 1: Adjektive zu Adverbien ▪

Bilde Adverbien und schreibe sie in dein Heft.

1. slow **2.** full **3.** careful **4.** crazy **5.** thirsty **6.** exact **7.** quick **8.** noisy
9. possible **10.** cruel **11.** happy **12.** terrible **13.** nervous **14.** angry
15. awful **16.** unhappy

Adjektiv oder Adverb?

Im Deutschen haben Adverbien keine besondere Endung, daher ist die Unterscheidung umso schwieriger. Man sagt zum Beispiel:

> Das Wetter ist schön. Sie singt schön.

„Schön" ist im ersten Satz Adjektiv, im zweiten Satz Adverb. Den Unterschied zeigt folgende Tabelle:

Adjektiv	Adverb
Adjektive beziehen sich auf **Nomen.**	**Adverbien** der Art und Weise beziehen sich auf **Verben.**
Hilfsfrage: Wie ist eine Sache/ Person beschaffen?	Hilfsfrage: Wie (auf welche Art und Weise) macht jemand etwas?
Pam is a **beautiful** young lady. They are very **careful**.	Pam sings **beautifully**. They carry the box **carefully**.

▪ Übung 2: Adjektiv oder Adverb? ▪

Welche Wortart ist richtig? Achte auf die Endungen.

1. Mr Graham is very angr_____, because Tom has dropped his

beautiful_____ flower pot. **2.** He shouts angr_____ at Tom,

"Why can't you be more careful_____?" **3.** Tom is unhapp_____.

He answers: "I'm sorry, I didn't hold the pot careful_____." **4.** Mr

Graham says, "You behaved terrib_____." **5.** Tom: "Well, next

time I'll carry it careful_____." **6.** Mr Graham is not angr_____

any more. He happ_____ invites Tom for a glass of lemonade.

7. Tom says thank you and drinks the lemonade thirst_____.

Tipp:
Manchmal ist keine weitere Endung nötig!

NOCH GEWUSST?

··

Zwischentest III

Für jeden
richtigen Satz
gibt es in beiden
Aufgaben
2 Punkte.

▪ Aufgabe 1: Ein Popstar ▪

Welches Wort passt in welche Lücke? Adjektiv oder Adverb?

famous – good – happily – loudly – nice – politely – quick – well – young

Deine Punktzahl:

(1) ___
(2) ___
(3) ___
(4) ___
(5) ___
(6) ___
(7) ___
(8) ___

Summe: ___

1. Johnny Guitar is a _____ pop star. **2.** He learned to play the guitar as a _____ boy. He was nine at the time. **3.** He is twenty-three now and he can play the instrument _____. **4.** He is a _____ singer, too. **5.** Even older people like him, because he does not play the guitar too _____. **6.** He and his band play _____ dances and _____ love songs. **7.** When a concert is over, Johnny _____ says thank you. **8.** The people who have listened to him clap their hands _____.

▪ Aufgabe 2: Wie war das noch? ▪

Deine Punktzahl:

(1) ___

(2) ___

(3) ___

(4) ___

Summe: ___

Trage die Vergleichswörter und die Steigerungsformen der Adjektive ein.

1. This film is not _____ terrible _____ I thought.

2. London is bigger _____ Berlin.

3. fantastic _____ _____

4. angry_____ _____

66

▪ Aufgabe 3: Nicht Wort für Wort ▪

Übertrage die folgenden Sätze ins Englische. Tipp: Achte auf die unterschiedliche Wortstellung im Deutschen und Englischen. Schreibe die Sätze in dein Heft.

1. Gestern war ich zu Hause *(at home)*. **2.** Wir waren letzte Woche *(last week)* in Berlin. **3.** Jennifer besuchte *(saw)* gestern ihre Oma *(grandma)*. **4.** Er aß in *(at)* „Billy's Diner" einen Hamburger. **5.** Er trank *(had)* mit zwei Freunden ein Glas Limonade *(a glass of lemonade)*. **6.** Du musst es ihr *(to her)* erzählen.

Für jeden richtigen Satz 3 Punkte.

Deine Punktzahl:

(1) ___
(2) ___
(3) ___
(4) ___
(5) ___
(6) ___

Summe: ___

▪ Aufgabe 4: Der Geheimcode ▪

Jack hat die Geheimzahl seines Tresors verlegt. Helfen wir ihm, indem wir die Wörter in die richtige Reihenfolge bringen. Erledige die Aufgabe in deinem Heft.

1. colour (1) – is (25) – what (19) – it (9) –?
2. out (9) – the (15) – snack (14) – bar (5) – of (19) – came (7) – he (14)
3. she (20) – on (14) – knocking (9) – door (1) – the (7) – is (8)
4. Gary (4) – us (15) – help (4) – can (14) –?
5. thief (8) – the (9) – on (20) – rides (1) – stolen (5) – away (15) – bike (18) – quickly (14) – a (8)

Für jeden richtigen Satz 2 Punkte.

Deine Punktzahl:

(1) ___

(2) ___

(3) ___

(4) ___

(5) ___

Summe: ___

Auf zum Endspurt.

DAS WAR'S

· ·

Abschlusstest

■ Aufgabe 1: Groß oder klein? ■

Curly, der Schlange, geht es gar nicht gut. Vor ihren Augen dreht sich alles, da sie kaum noch die Buchstaben erkennen kann. Du siehst mehr. Schreibe die Sätze in korrekter Groß- und Kleinschreibung in dein Heft.

Tipp: Setze ebenfalls Punkte und andere Satzzeichen. Vergiss auch nicht Apostrophe.

Für jedes richtige Satzzeichen gibt es einen Punkt, für jede richtige Großschreibung (außer am Satzanfang) 2 Punkte.

▪ Aufgabe 2: Eine nicht ganz alltägliche Geschichte ▪

Mrs Price erzählt von einigen Gästen. Ersetze die englischen Nomen durch die richtigen Pluralformen. Verwende die richtigen Pronomen und Kurzformen.

1. You know, yesterday, Snappy, _____ *(mein)* dog, was barking. **2.** He didn't see _____ *(irgendwelche, keine)* _____ *(mouse).* **3.** There were three _____ *(child)* in _____ *(mein)* garden. **4.** _____ *(sie)* were looking at the apple-tree. **5.** I did not _____ *(short form)* know _____ *(diese)* young _____ *(people).*

6. Well, I was a little bit afraid. You hear a lot of _____ *(story)* about stupid _____ *(thing)* _____ *(teenager)* do. **7.** *(Mein)* _____ good old Snappy, an Irish setter, ran towards them. **8.** Two boys were looking at the apple-tree. One of them was shouting _____ *(etwas)* which I could not _____ *(short form)* understand.

9. I went out of the house at once and said to Snappy, "Stop it!" Then I saw one of the boys in _____ *(mein)* apple-tree. **10.** I shouted at him, "_____ *(was)* are _____ *(du)* doing there?" **11.** The boy was shocked when he heard _____ *(diese)* words. **12.** Oh no! _____ *(er)* fell off the tree. **13.** But _____ *(er)* did not _____ *(short form)* fall far. **14.** Then I could see that he had a cat in _____ *(seinen)* arms. **15.** The children said to _____ *(ihrem)* friend, "_____ *(du)* saved Fay's life."

Für jede richtige Lösung erhältst du 1 Punkt. Zähle die Punkte pro Satz zusammen.

Deine Punktzahl:

(1) ___

(2) ___

(3) ___

(4) ___

(5) ___

(6) ___

(7) ___

(8) ___

(9) ___

(10) ___

(11) ___

(12) ___

(13) ___

(14) ___

(15) ___

Summe: 10

▪ Aufgabe 3: Richtig? ▪

Für jeden richtig verbesserten Satz gibt es 2 Punkte.

Welcher der beiden unterstrichenen Satzteile ist jeweils falsch? Kreuze den Buchstaben an und schreibe die richtige Lösung in dein Heft.

Deine Punktzahl:

(1) ___

(2) ___

(3) ___

(4) ___

(5) ___

(6) ___

(7) ___

(8) ___

(9) ___

(10) ___

(11) ___

(12) ___

(13) ___

(14) ___

(15) ___

(16) ___

Summe: ___

1. The (a) <u>holidays</u> (b) <u>begun</u> yesterday, on June, 15. **2.** The (a) <u>Webster's</u> went to Sevilla in Spain to spend their holidays (b) <u>there.</u> **3.** (a) <u>Their</u> house in Baker Street was empty, only the (b) <u>Bakers</u> cats were in the shed behind the house. **4.** The Hooks, (a) <u>there</u> neighbours, (b) <u>looked</u> after the cats every Tuesday, Thursday and Saturday. **5.** Laura, (a) the <u>Hooks'</u> youngest daughter, (b) <u>arrive</u> at the house on Thursday. **6.** When she (a) <u>come</u> to the back door, she (b) <u>saw</u> that a window was broken. **7.** She said to herself, "Maybe I (a) <u>have left</u> it open yesterday, or maybe (b) <u>Mum</u> didn't close it when she was here. **8.** Laura (a) <u>opened</u> the door and went (b) <u>careful</u> into the house. **9.** When she (a) <u>was</u> in the living-room, she (b) <u>stoped</u> for a while, because she could hear a loud noise. **10.** It was … yes, she could hear it from the kitchen, two (a) <u>babys</u> were (b) <u>crying.</u> **11.** (a) <u>Quick,</u> she (b) <u>ran</u> to the kitchen door, but she didn't open it at once. **12.** She (a) <u>was</u> afraid, because she couldn't hear (b) <u>something</u> then. **13.** But (a) <u>then</u> she went in and didn't (b) <u>wanted</u> to believe her eyes: What a mess in the kitchen! **14.** (a) <u>Potatos</u> were on the floor, (b) <u>milk</u> was on the kitchen table, a cookbook was on a chair. **15.** And (a) <u>then</u> … believe it or not, there were two kittens in a string bag *(Einkaufsnetz)*. Strings from the net were round their (b) <u>foots</u> and their necks. They couldn't get out of it. **16.** Laura (a) <u>helped</u> the kittens to get out of the net. Then she gave them some milk. They drank (b) <u>thirsty.</u>

70

■ Aufgabe 4: Adjektiv- und Adverbrätsel ■

Achte genau auf die Aufgabenstellungen. Setze dann die richtigen Wörter ein.

Tipp: Hier sind einige schwierige Adjektive: busy, careful, cruel (grausam).

Für jede richtige Lösung gibt es 1 Punkt.

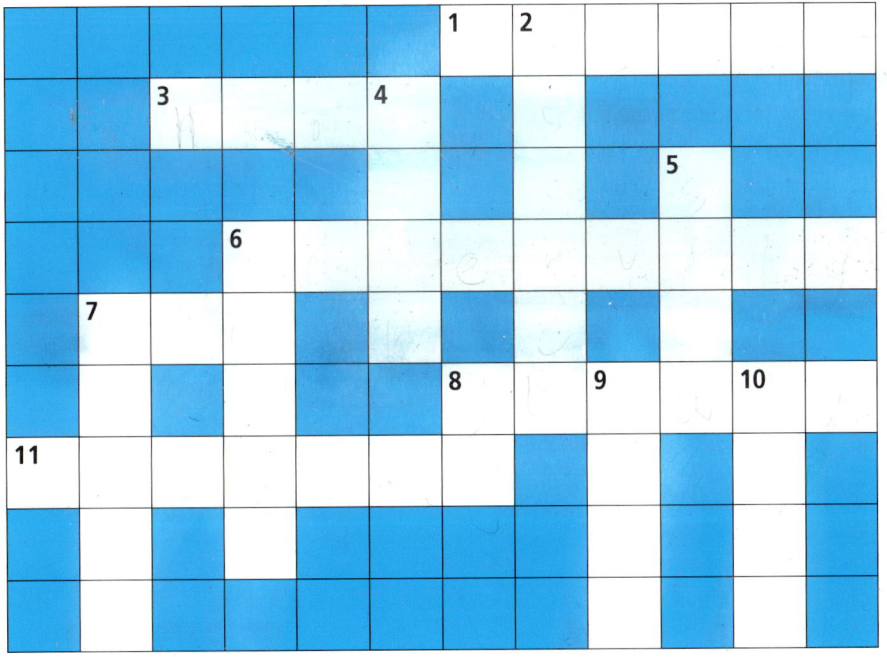

Geschafft! Hoch lebe der Grammatik-Champion.

ACROSS (waagerecht): **1.** They work a lot, they work b… **3.** Life is not easy, it is h… **6.** You do not want to break anything, so you carry it c… **7.** The opposite of near. **8.** The car does not move quickly, it moves s… **11.** The monster is not nice, it behaves c…

DOWN (senkrecht): **2.** Something you like to use and which really helps you is a u… thing. **4.** When you can't see anything, it is d… **5.** The old car is not quick, it is s… **6.** The monster is not nice, it is c… **7.** 40 in letters. **9.** The opposite of closed. **10.** The opposite of early.

LÖSUNGEN

Seite 10 / 11

Teil A: 1. F, an; 2. F, children; 3. F, hobbies; 4. F, people; 5. R; 6. F, Peter's; 7. R; 8. R; 9. F, English; 10. F, T-shirts.
Bei mehr als einer falschen Antwort solltest du Kapitel 4, „Nomen", durcharbeiten.

Teil B: 11. F, We are; 12. F, their books; 13. F, Its colour; 14. R; 15. R; 16. F, Whose; 17. R; 18. F, Which sweat shirt.
Bei mehr als einer falschen Antwort bitte Kapitel 5, „Pronomen", durcharbeiten.

Teil C: 19. F, best; 20. F, not as good as; 21. F, more terrible, most terrible; 22. R.
Bei mehr als einer falschen Antwort Kapitel 11, „Adjektive", erarbeiten.

Teil D: 23. F, coming; 24. F, said; 25. F, We saw; 26. F, She took; 27. F, dropped; 28. F, has not gone; 29. F, cannot; 30. R; 31. R.
Bei mehr als einer falschen Antwort Kapitel 7, „Verben und Zeiten", lernen.

Teil E: 32. F, Can you help me?; 33. R; 34. F, Who wears; 35. F, Where do; 36. F, How much.
Bei mehr als einer falschen Antwort bitte Kapitel 8, „Fragen und Antworten", durcharbeiten.

Teil F: 37. F, I went home at 8 o'clock; 38. F, Do you come; 39. F, Our cat has / drinks milk every day; 40. R.
Bei mehr als einer falschen Antwort solltest du Kapitel 10, „Satzbau", durcharbeiten.

Teil G: 41. R; 42 F, played well; 43. R; 44. F, carefully.
Bei mehr als einer falschen Antwort die Regeln in Kapitel 12, „Adverbien", lernen.

Seite 12

Übung 1: Folgende Kästchen müssen rot ausgemalt werden: 1. Henry / dog; 2. school; 3. Mike / London; 4. sister / hamster; 5. parents / TV; 6. Larry; 7. Linda / bike.

Übung 2: 1. John; 2. biro, table; 3. Jack, school-bag; 4. taxi; 5. cat, sofa; 6. window; 7. water, glass; 8. father, house.

Seite 13

Übung 3: 1. an; 2. a; 3. a; 4. an; 5. A; 6. an.

Übung 4: Folgende Sätze müssen markiert werden: 2, 4, 5.

Seite 14

Übung 5: 1. windows, 2. sisters, 3. countries, 4. boys, 5. taxis, 6. friends, 7. girls, 8. toys, 9. bushes, 10. chips, 11. diaries, 12. hamsters, 13. dresses, 14. kisses, 15. hobbies, 16. shirts, 17. rivers, 18. teddies, 19. bottles, 20. circuses.

Übung 6: „-s": 3. book, 4. key, 7. cowboy, 8. pencil, 10. hammer. „-ies": 1. diary, 2. teddy, 9. pony. „-es": 5. brush, 6. blouse.

Seite 15

Übung 7: 1. windows; 2. toys; 3. men, women, children; 4. pages, 5. families; 6. people.

Seite 16

Übung 8: 1. Mr Smith's car; 2. Mrs Jackson's sports car; 3. Kate's exercise book; 4. The hamster's food; 5. Jenny's new trousers; 6. The Ryans' caravan; 7. The two budgies' cage; 8. The grocer's children.

Seite 17
Übung 9: 1. My friend's mother; 2. The wheel of the go-cart; 3. My friend's comic; 4. Paul's classroom; 5. the colour of his socks.

Seite 18
Übung 10: 1. English; 2. August; 3. table; 4. window; 5. Christmas; 6. T-shirt; 7. book; 8. Biology.

Seite 19
Übung 11: 1. My name is Jenny Jenkins. 2. You know, I come from Scotland. 3. My mother is from Germany. 4. We are in Tutzingen now, a nice little German town. 5. Look here! This is a T-shirt from Tutzingen. I love it.

Übung 12: 1. DJ; 2. November; 3. pen / pencil / biro; 4. Christmas; 5. school-bag; 6. T-shirt; 7. TV; 8. English.

Übung 13: We are in France this year. 2. It is August 15th. 3. The weather is very sunny. 4. We swim a lot.

Seite 21
Übung 14: three cups of tea (milk); many children; a bucket of water (milk); a bottle of lemonade (milk, water); some salt; two glasses of milk (lemonade, water); five slices of bread; a bar of chocolate.

Pronomen

Seite 23
Übung 1: 1. They; 2. He; 3. She; 4. It; 5. They; 6. He; 7. It; 8. They.

Übung 2: 1. It; 2. you; 3. I; 4. you – We; 5. They; 6. It; 7. She; 8. He; 9. They; 10. She.

Seite 24
Übung 3: 1. my, your; 2. his; 3. her; 4. your, Our, our; 5. their; 6. Its; 7. Its; 8. Her; 9. His; 10. Their.

Seite 25
Übung 4: 1. some; 2. any; 3. some; 4. any; 5. some; 6. somewhere; 7. anybody; 8. anything.

Seite 26
Übung 5: 1. This, that; 2. these; 3. those; 4. this, these, those, those.

Seite 27
Übung 6: 1. this bag; 2. this box; 3. this walkman; 4. these books; 5. these sweets; 6. this car; 7. these apples; 8. this ball; 9. this goldfish; 10. these budgies; 11. that picture; 12. those pencils; 13. those magazines; 14. that dog; 15. that cassette-recorder; 16. those cassettes; 17. that cat; 18. that biro; 19. that cap; 20. those cameras.

Seite 28
Übung 7: 1. Where; 2. What; 3. When; 4. Whose; 5. How; 6. What; 7. How; 8. What; 9. Where; 10. Who; 11. How; 12. Whose

Seite 29
Übung 8: 1. What; 2. Which; 3. What; 4. What; 5. Which; 6. Which.

Zwischentest I

Seite 30
Aufgabe 1: 1. geese, 2. cats, 3. mice, 4. flowers, 5. fish, 6. tomatoes.

Aufgabe 2: 1. Sharon's bike; 2. The Jacksons' car; 3. The windows of the house; 4. Mr Miller's team; 5. The wheels of the go-cart.

Auswertung Aufgaben 1 und 2: 22 Punkte: ausgezeichnet; 20 Punkte: gut; 18 Punkte: nicht schlecht; 16 Punkte: na ja; 14 Punkte und weniger: Kapitel 4, „Nomen", wiederholen.

Seite 31
Aufgabe 3: 1. my; 2. I; 3. It; 4. their; 5. they; 6. Her; 7. You.
Aufgabe 4: 1. Who; 2. Where; 3. What; 4. Which; 5. Why; 6. When.
Auswertung Aufgaben 3 und 4: 26 Punkte: ausgezeichnet; 24 Punkte: gut; 22 Punkte: nicht schlecht; 18–20 Punkte: na ja; 16 Punkte und weniger: Kapitel 5, „Pronomen", wiederholen.

Verben und Zeiten

Seite 32
Übung 1: 1. help; 2. say**s**; 3. put**s**; 4. sing; 5. understand; 6. go**es**; 7. cr**ies**; 8. drive**s**; 9. go; 10. run**s**.

Seite 33
Übung 2: 1. get**s** up; 2. arrive**s**; 3. start**s**; 4. have lunch; 5. is; 6. play.
Übung 3: 1. goes; 2. flies; 3. says; 4. drives; 5. has; 6. cries; 7. is; 8. does; 9. has; 10. watches.

Seite 34
Übung 4: 1. is reading; 2. are watching; 3. are playing; 4. am doing; 5. is opening; 6. is asking.

Seite 35
Übung 5: 1. coming; 2. going; 3. beginning; 4. taking; 5. sitting; 6. reading; 7. writing; 8. running; 9. crying; 10. shouting; 11. lying; 12. cycling.
Übung 6: 1. is writing; 2. are playing; 3. are swimming; 4. is kicking; 5. is running; 6. are having; 7. are dancing; 8. is tying.

Seite 36 / 37
Übung 7: *Bild 1:* This is Bonny, Brenda's dog. Bonny likes the red ball. *Bild 2:* Every day, Brenda and Bonny play in the garden. Look! Today, the sun is shining. Bonny is playing with the ball. *Bild 3:* Brenda's mother says, "Please go to the supermarket and buy some milk, OK?" *Bild 4:* Look! Brenda and Bonny are walking down the street. *Bild 5:* Suddenly Bonny sees a cat. Bonny tries / is trying to catch it. *Bild 6:* The man on the bike stops. Now apples and other things fall / are falling out of the basket. The man is angry. *Bild 7:* A car stops. A woman goes over to Brenda. The woman is angry, too. *Bild 8:* Bonny and the cat come back. The woman is happy. She says to Brenda, "This is Tilly, my cat. I'm so happy." *Bild 9:* Brenda says sorry to the man. The woman is laughing. She is looking at her cat.

Seite 38
Übung 8: 1. loved; 2. emptied; 3. stopped; 4. counted; 5. called; 6. dropped; 7. cried; 8. collected; 9. carried; 10. cycled.

Seite 39
Übung 9: 1. is, was; 2. went; 3. saw; 4. looked; 5. had; 6. took; 7. shows; 8. visited; 9. did; 10. thinks, is.

Seite 40
Übung 10: 1. is not (isn't); 2. do not eat (don't eat); 3. does not like (doesn't like); 4. has not got (hasn't got); 5. may not; 6. does not collect (doesn't collect); 7. do not clean (don't clean); 8. do not eat (don't eat); 9. have not got (haven't got).

Seite 41
Übung 11: 1. was not / wasn't; 2. has not got / hasn't got; 3. were not / weren't; 4. did not

watch / didn't watch; 5. did not open / didn't open; 6. did not buy / didn't buy; 7. is not watching / isn't watching; 8. could not open / couldn't open; 9. cannot come / can't come; 10. does not put on / doesn't put on.

Seite 42

Übung 12: 1. They've bought; 2. She's put; 3. They've gone; 4. They've cycled; 5. They haven't been; 6. They've stopped; 7. He hasn't taken; 8. He hasn't been; 9. They've had; 10. They haven't had.

Seite 43

Übung 13: *Flugzeug 1:* a) we have run, b) I have written, c) he has not kept, d) you have taken, e) she has found, f) they have not said *Flugzeug 2:* a) I've done, b) we've thought, c) he hasn't played, d) she's had, e) he hasn't fallen, f) she's got.

Seite 44

Übung 14: 1. PAST; 2. NOW; 3. NOW; 4. PAST; 5. PAST; 6. NOW.

Seite 45

Übung 15: 1. (He) Tom has cycled. 2. (She) Sheila has written a letter. 3. (They) The children have played basketball. 4. Mrs Price (She) has called a taxi. 5. He (Barky) has run after a cat. 6. She (Janet) has watched TV.

Seite 46

Übung 16: 1. (1) 2. (2) 3. (2) 4. (3) 5. (1) oder (2) 6. (3).

Seite 47

Übung 17: 1. She'll (She will) go; 2. Mary and Jane will work; 3. We won't (We will not) cry; 4. John will play; 5. He'll (He will) drive; 6. Mr Smith will help; 7. The weather will be; 8. You will not (won't) be; 9. They'll (They will) have

got; 10. Mrs Thompson won't (will not) answer.

Übung 18: 1. will be; 2. won't be; 3. will take; 4. We'll see; 5. will say; 6. won't be; 7. will translate; 8. will help; 9. I'll live; 10. won't be, will be.

Seite 48

Übung 19: This afternoon she's (she is) going to buy a birthday present for Caren; 2. At five o'clock, she's (she is) going to tidy up her room. 3. Tomorrow she's (she is) going to repair Ben's bike. 4. At the weekend, she's (she is) going to be at her grandparents'. 5. Next Monday, she's (she is) going to play football; 6. Today at six o'clock, she's (she is) going to help her mother in the kitchen.

Seite 49

Übung 20: 1. 'll (will); 2. 'm (am) going to; 3. 'll (will); 4. will; 5. 's (is) going to; 6. are going to; 7. 'll (will) ('m going to/am going to).

Fragen und Antworten

Seite 50

Übung 1: 1. Does Robert play football? 2. Do the girls go to Glasgow? 3. Do the children read many books? 4. Can Robert play the piano? 5. Is Mildred here? 6. Does Betty like cats?

Seite 51

Übung 2: 1. Does the President play the guitar? 2. Does his wife work in the garden every day? 3. Do his children get up every morning at 6 o'clock? 4. Do the President's parents live in Memphis? 5. Why does the President fly to Paris every year? 6. What do the President's friends eat at a party? 7. Does the President's daughter ride a horse? 8. Do the President and his wife like Country & Western music? 9. Can the President speak German and French? 10. What does the President eat when there is a meeting?

Seite 52
Übung 3: 1. No, he isn't. 2. Yes, they can. 3. Yes, he is. 4. No, she doesn't. 5. Yes, they are. 6. No, they don't. 7. Yes, he can.

Seite 53
Übung 4: 1. she does; 2. we aren't; 3. they are; 4. I'm not; 5. they do; 6. we are; 7. he doesn't; 8. we do.

Zwischentest II

Seite 54
Aufgabe 1: 1. Kate is riding …; 2. The train is stopping …; 3. You are writing …? / Are you writing …?; 4. I'm getting tired; 5. What is lying there?; 6. … they are having …
Auswertung: 11–12 Punkte: sehr gut; 9–10 Punkte: gut; 7–8 Punkte: nicht schlecht; 6 und weniger als 6 Punkte: Present Progressive wiederholen.
Aufgabe 2: 1. ringing; 2. answers; 3. can; 4. talking; 5. wants; 6. likes; 7. asks; coming; 8. answers; want; 9. hears; says; 10. dancing; likes.
Auswertung: 13–14 Punkte: sehr gut; 11–12 Punkte: gut; 9–10 Punkte: nicht schlecht; 7–8 Punkte: na ja; weniger als 7 Punkte: Simple Present und Present Progressive wiederholen.

Seite 55
Aufgabe 3: 1. is shining; 2. are having; 3. ask; 4. says; 5. take, go; 6. throws; 7. throw; 8. are having; 9. is flying; 10. swooshes, lands; 11. gets; 12. runs; 13. run; 14. can; 15. look; 16. has; 17. says, play; 18. gives.
Auswertung: 20–21 Punkte: sehr gut;

17–19 Punkte: gut; 14–16 Punkte nicht schlecht; 13–15 Punkte: geht so; weniger als 13 Punkte: Wiederholung Present Progressive und Simple Present.

Seite 56
Aufgabe 4: 1. is; 2. is; 3. has already invited; 4. has sent; 5. made; 6. is; 7. are waiting; 8. say; 9. give; 10. likes; 11. asked; 12. know; have bought.
Auswertung: 12–13 Punkte: sehr gut; 10–11 Punkte: gut; 8–9 Punkte: nicht schlecht; 7 Punkte und weniger: Simple Present, Present Progressive, Present Perfect und Simple Past wiederholen.
Aufgabe 5: 1. is going to visit; 2. is going to work; 3. is going to learn; 4. Will I be; 5. Will I meet; 6. Will I win.
Auswertung: 6 Punkte: sehr gut; 5 Punkte: gut; 4 Punkte: nicht schlecht; 3 Punkte und weniger: Going-to- und Will-Future wiederholen.

Seite 57
Aufgabe 6: 1. Where; 2. it was; 3. What; 4. we didn't; 5. we did; 6. we don't; 7. Why; 8. Whose.
Auswertung: 8 Punkte: sehr gut; 7 Punkte: gut; 6 Punkte: nicht schlecht; 5 Punkte und weniger: Fragewörter und Kurzantworten wiederholen.

Satzbau

Seite 58
Übung 1: 1. Jennifer has got a nice new blouse. 2. They talk to them. 3. John is playing with his dog. 4. Anne is reading a book. 5. The children are having a party. 6. Jenny has got her new cap on. 7. Many British schoolchildren wear school uniforms. 8. Snuffy does not like dog biscuits.

Seite 59

Übung 2: 1. MacCool plays basketball in the evening. 2. Mr Paulsen watched TV in the hotel in the evening. 3. Pat helps her father in the kitchen in the afternoon. 4. The Wilsons eat an apple every evening. 5. Christine cycles along the river in the afternoon. 6. Mrs Paulsen wrote a letter in the living-room in the evening. 7. Mr Jennings looked at the pictures on the table after lunch. 8. Sarah and Toby put a bottle of milk on the table after shopping. 9. Mrs Potter went with her dog to the park in the afternoon. 10. The children in 6c sang a song at 10 o'clock.

Adjektive

Seite 60

Übung 1: 1. big – bigger – biggest 2. tall – taller – tallest 3. modern – more modern – most modern 4. hungry – hungrier – hungriest 5. thin – thinner – thinnest 6. famous – more famous – most famous.

Seite 61

Übung 2: 1. Spot's house is as big as Fang's house. 2. Suzy is not as wet as Flag. 3. The water is hotter than the lemonade. 4. A lion is more dangerous than a cat. 5. London is bigger than Berlin.

Seite 62

Übung 3: short, shorter, shortest; young, younger, youngest; good, better, best; small, smaller, smallest; funny, funnier, funniest; hot, hotter, hottest; bad, worse, worst; dangerous, more dangerous, most dangerous; terrible, more terrible, most terrible; lucky, luckier, luckiest; wet, wetter, wettest; famous, more famous, most famous.

Seite 63

Übung 4: 1. In New York, (the) houses are higher. 2. In New York, there are more cars. 3. In New York, (the) streets are noisier and dirtier. 4. In the village, (the) people are poorer. 5. In New York, (the) shops are bigger than in the village. 6. In the village, (the) streets are quieter. 7. New York is not as exciting as the village. 8. In the village (, there) are more trees than in New York. 9. In the village, (the) streets are not as wide as in New York. 10. In the village, (the) people are friendlier than in New York.

Adverbien der Art und Weise

Seite 64

Übung 1: 1. slowly 2. fully 3. carefully 4. crazily 5. thirstily 6. exactly 7. quickly 8. noisily 9. possibly 10. cruelly 11. happily 12. terribly 13. nervously 14. angrily 15. awfully 16. unhappily.

Seite 65

Übung 2: 1. angry, beautiful; 2. angrily, careful; 3. unhappy, carefully; 4. terribly; 5. carefully; 6. angry; happily; 7. thirstily.

Zwischentest III

Seite 66

Aufgabe 1: 1. famous; 2. young; 3. well; 4. good; 5. loudly; 6. quick, nice; 7. politely; 8. happily.

Aufgabe 2: 1. as … as; 2. than; 3. fantastic, more fantastic, most fantastic; 4. angry, angrier, angriest.

Auswertung der Aufgaben 1 und 2: 24 Punkte ausgezeichnet; 22–23 Punkte: gut; 20–21

Punkte: nicht schlecht; 17–19 Punkte: na ja;
16 Punkte und weniger: Die Kapitel „Adjektive" und „Adverbien" unbedingt wiederholen.

Seite 67

Aufgabe 3: 1. I was at home yesterday.
2. We were in Berlin last week (Last week, we
were in Berlin). 3. Jennifer saw her grandma
yesterday. 4. He ate a hamburger at "Billy's
Diner". 5. He had a glass of lemonade with
two friends. 6. You must tell it to her.
Aufgabe 4: 1. What colour is it? 2. He came
out of the snack bar. 3. She is knocking on the
door. 4. Can Gary help us? 5. The thief rides
quickly away on a stolen bike.
Auswertung der Aufgaben 3 und 4: 28 Punkte:
ausgezeichnet; 23–27 Punkte: gut;
18–22 Punkte: nicht schlecht; 13–17 Punkte:
na ja; weniger als 13 Punkte: Unbedingt Kapitel
„Satzbau" wiederholen. *Die Geheimzahl lautet
also 191259 / 14791915145 / 20891471 /
144415 / 9811415208518. Kein Wunder, dass
Jack sie vergessen hatte!*

Abschlusstest

Seite 68

Aufgabe 1: Hello, **(1)** Curly. **(1)** Are you an
English **(2)** snake**? (1)** Do you come from
London **(2)** ? **(1)** I live in **S**ydney **(2)**. **(1)** It's **(1)**
in **A**ustralia **(2)**. **(1)** I like to turn round**. (1)** But
I (2) don't **(1)** like to watch **TV (2)**. **(1)** I also
like to listen to **CD'**s **(2 + 1), (1)** because they
turn round like me**. (1)**
Auswertung: 25–27 Punkte: sehr gut;
22–24 Punkte: gut; 18–21 Punkte: nicht
schlecht; 14–17 Punkte: na ja; weniger als
14 Punkte: Kapitel 4, „Groß- und Kleinschreibung", durcharbeiten.

Seite 69

Aufgabe 2: 1. my; 2. any, mice; 3. children,
my; 4. They; 5. didn't, these, people; 6. stories,
things, teenagers; 7. My; 8. something,
couldn't; 9. my; 10. What, you; 11. these;
12. He; 13. he, didn't; 14. his; 15. their, You.
Auswertung: 25 Punkte: ausgezeichnet;
22–24 Punkte: gut; 18–21 Punkte: nicht
schlecht; 14–17 Punkte: na ja; weniger als
14 Punkte: auf jeden Fall Kapitel 4, Nomen,
und das 5. Kapitel, Pronomen, wiederholen.

Seite 70

Aufgabe 3: *Richtig wären:* 1. (b) began; 2. (a)
Websters; 3. (b) Bakers'; 4. (a) their; 5. (b)
arrived; 6. (a) came; 7. (a) left; 8. (b) carefully;
9. (b) stopped; 10. (a) babies; 11. (a) Quickly;
12. (b) anything; 13. (b) want; 14. (a) Potatoes;
15. (b) feet; 16. (b) thirstily.
Auswertung: 31–32 Punkte: sehr gut;
26–30 Punkte: gut; 21–25 Punkte: nicht
schlecht; 18–20 Punkte: na ja; weniger als
18 Punkte: Eine Wiederholung der fehlerträch-
tigsten Kapitel (Simple Past, Present Perfect:
Sätze Nr. 1, 5, 6, 7, 9, 13; Nomen: Sätze Nr. 2,
10, 14, 15; Genitiv: Satz Nr. 3; Pronomen: Sätze
Nr. 4, 12; Adverbien: Sätze Nr. 8, 11, 16) ist
unbedingt notwendig.

Seite 71

Aufgabe 4: ACROSS: 1. busily; 3. hard;
6. carefully; 7. far; 8. slowly; 11. cruelly.
DOWN: 2. useful; 4. dark; 5. slow; 6. cruel;
7. forty; 9. open; 10. late
Auswertung: 12–13 Punkte: sehr gut;
10–11 Punkte: gut; 8–9 Punkte: nicht schlecht;
6–7 Punkte: na ja; weniger als 6 Punkte:
Wiederholung des 12. Kapitels, Adverbien

In der Reihe FALKEN Schülerhilfe sind zahlreiche Titel erschienen.
Überall erhältlich, wo es Bücher gibt.

Dieses Buch wurde auf chlorfrei gebleichtem und säurefreiem Papier gedruckt.

Der Text dieses Buches entspricht der neuen deutschen Rechtschreibung.

ISBN 3 8068 2108 9

© 1998 by FALKEN Verlag, 65527 Niedernhausen/Ts.
Umschlaggestaltung: Peter Udo Pinzer
Gestaltung: Horst Bachmann
Redaktion: Dr. Petra Begemann
Titelgrafiken und Zeichnungen: Jovica Savin, Frankfurt am Main
Fotos: Bildagentur Huber, Garmisch-Partenkirchen: 57 (R. Schmid); **Britische Zentrale für Fremdenverkehr,** Frankfurt a.M.: 39; **dpa,** Frankfurt a.M.: 51 (European Press); **FALKEN Archiv:** 20 oben (TLC), 20 Mitte (Eichler/Hofmann), 20 unten (U. Kopp); **Das Fotoarchiv,** Essen: 13 (T. Babovic), 17 (K. Müller), 49 (H. Christoph); **Keystone Pressedienst,** Hamburg: 60; **laenderpress,** Düsseldorf: 23 (C. Voigt), 63 links (HEMO); **Reinhard-Tierfoto,** Heiligkreuzsteinach-Eiterbach: 70; **Silvestris Fotoservice,** Kastl/Obb.: 15, 63 rechts (F. Lane).

Die Ratschläge in diesem Buch sind von dem Autor und vom Verlag sorgfältig erwogen und geprüft, dennoch kann eine Garantie nicht übernommen werden. Eine Haftung des Autors bzw. des Verlags und seiner Beauftragten für Personen-, Sach- und Vermögensschäden ist ausgeschlossen.

Satz: Raasch & Partner GmbH, Neu-Isenburg
Druck: Ludwig Auer GmbH, Donauwörth

817 2635 4453 6271

Schulsorgen?

Neben dieser Buchreihe bietet die Schülerhilfe, Deutschlands große Nachhilfe-Organisation, einen regelmäßigen Förderunterricht. Dort gibt's qualifizierte Hausaufgaben-Betreuung in kleinen Gruppen und preiswerte Nachhilfe ab der Grundschule. Schülerhilfen finden Sie in vielen deutschen Städten.

Wählen Sie unsere bundeseinheitliche Telefon-Nr. 19418 montags bis freitags von 15.00 bis 17.30 Uhr.

(Ganztagsauskunft unter 0209/19418)

Schülerhilfe ®

Lernen macht wieder Spaß

▪ Aufgabe 4: Adjektiv- und Adverbrätsel ▪

Achte genau auf die Aufgabenstellungen. Setze dann die richtigen Wörter ein.

Tipp: Hier sind einige schwierige Adjektive: busy, careful, cruel (grausam).

Für jede richtige Lösung gibt es 1 Punkt.

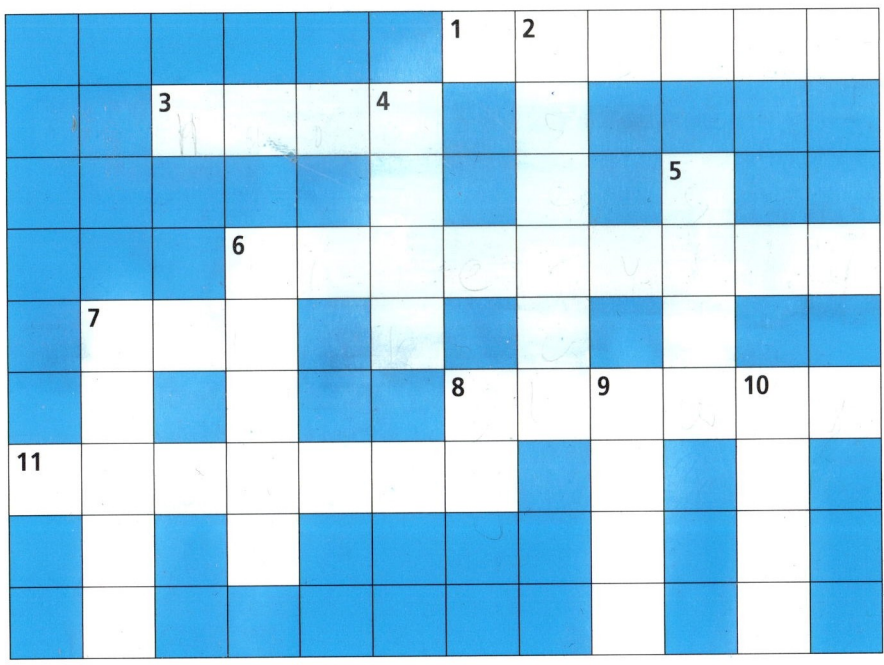

Geschafft! Hoch lebe der Grammatik-Champion.

ACROSS (waagerecht): **1.** They work a lot, they work b… **3.** Life is not easy, it is h… **6.** You do not want to break anything, so you carry it c… **7.** The opposite of near. **8.** The car does not move quickly, it moves s… **11.** The monster is not nice, it behaves c…

DOWN (senkrecht): **2.** Something you like to use and which really helps you is a u… thing. **4.** When you can't see anything, it is d… **5.** The old car is not quick, it is s… **6.** The monster is not nice, it is c… **7.** 40 in letters. **9.** The opposite of closed. **10.** The opposite of early.

LÖSUNGEN

··

Seite 10 / 11

Teil A: 1. F, an; 2. F, children; 3. F, hobbies;
4. F, people; 5. R; 6. F, Peter's; 7. R; 8. R;
9. F, English; 10. F, T-shirts.
Bei mehr als einer falschen Antwort solltest du
Kapitel 4, „Nomen", durcharbeiten.
Teil B: 11. F, We are; 12. F, their books;
13. F, Its colour; 14. R; 15. R; 16. F, Whose;
17. R; 18. F, Which sweat shirt.
Bei mehr als einer falschen Antwort bitte
Kapitel 5, „Pronomen", durcharbeiten.
Teil C: 19. F, best; 20. F, not as good as;
21. F, more terrible, most terrible; 22. R.
Bei mehr als einer falschen Antwort Kapitel 11,
„Adjektive", erarbeiten.
Teil D: 23. F, coming; 24. F, said; 25. F, We saw;
26. F, She took; 27. F, dropped; 28. F, has not
gone; 29. F, cannot; 30. R; 31. R.
Bei mehr als einer falschen Antwort Kapitel 7,
„Verben und Zeiten", lernen.
Teil E: 32. F, Can you help me?; 33. R; 34. F,
Who wears; 35. F, Where do; 36. F, How much.
Bei mehr als einer falschen Antwort bitte
Kapitel 8, „Fragen und Antworten", durchar-
beiten.
Teil F: 37. F, I went home at 8 o'clock; 38. F,
Do you come; 39. F, Our cat has / drinks milk
every day; 40. R.
Bei mehr als einer falschen Antwort solltest du
Kapitel 10, „Satzbau", durcharbeiten.
Teil G: 41. R; 42 F, played well; 43. R; 44. F,
carefully.
Bei mehr als einer falschen Antwort die Regeln
in Kapitel 12, „Adverbien", lernen.

Seite 12

Übung 1: Folgende Kästchen müssen rot
ausgemalt werden: 1. Henry / dog; 2. school;
3. Mike / London; 4. sister / hamster; 5. parents /
TV; 6. Larry; 7. Linda / bike.
Übung 2: 1. John; 2. biro, table; 3. Jack,
school-bag; 4. taxi; 5. cat, sofa; 6. window;
7. water, glass; 8. father, house.

Seite 13

Übung 3: 1. an; 2. a; 3. a; 4. an; 5. A; 6. an.
Übung 4: Folgende Sätze müssen markiert
werden: 2, 4, 5.

Seite 14

Übung 5: 1. windows, 2. sisters, 3. countries,
4. boys, 5. taxis, 6. friends, 7. girls, 8. toys,
9. bushes, 10. chips, 11. diaries, 12. hamsters,
13. dresses, 14. kisses, 15. hobbies, 16. shirts,
17. rivers, 18. teddies, 19. bottles, 20. circuses.
Übung 6: „-s": 3. book, 4. key, 7. cowboy,
8. pencil, 10. hammer. „-ies": 1. diary, 2. teddy,
9. pony. „-es": 5. brush, 6. blouse.

Seite 15

Übung 7: 1. windows; 2. toys; 3. men, women,
children; 4. pages, 5. families; 6. people.

Seite 16

Übung 8: 1. Mr Smith's car; 2. Mrs Jackson's
sports car; 3. Kate's exercise book; 4. The
hamster's food; 5. Jenny's new trousers;
6. The Ryans' caravan; 7. The two budgies'
cage; 8. The grocer's children.